Communicating

with e-mail and the Internet

Learning Made Simple

P.K. McBride

Routledge
Taylor & Francis Group

LONDON AND NEW YORK

First published 2006 by Elsevier Ltd.

2 Park Square, Milton Park, Abingdon, Oxon OX14 4RN
711 Third Avenue, New York, NY 10017, USA

Routledge is an imprint of the Taylor & Francis Group, an informa business

First issued in hardback 2017

First edition 2006

British Library Cataloguing in Publication Data
A catalogue record for this book is available from the British Library

ISBN-13: 978-0-7506-8189-6 (pbk)
ISBN-13: 978-1-138-43630-5 (hbk)

 Typeset by P.K. McBride

Icons designed by Sarah Ward © 1994

Transferred to Digital Print 2011

Contents

Preface

The books in the Learning Made Simple series aim to do exactly what it says on the cover – make learning simple.

A Learning Made Simple book:

◆ Is **fully illustrated**: with clearly labelled screenshots.

◆ Is **easy to read**: with brief explanations, and clear instructions.

◆ Is **task-based**: each short section concentrates on one job at a time.

◆ **Builds knowledge**: ideas and techniques are presented in the right order so that your understanding builds progressively as you work through the book.

◆ Is **flexible**: as each section is self-contained, if you know it, you can skip it.

The books in the Learning Made Simple books series are designed with learning in mind, and so do not directly follow the structure of any specific syllabus – but they do cover the content. This book covers Module 7 of the ECDL syllabus and Units 7 and 8 of New CLAIT. For details of how the sections map against your syllabus, please go to the web site:

http://www.madesimple.co.uk

1 The Internet

The Net and the Web

Let's start by clearing up a common confusion – the Internet and the World Wide Web are not the same thing.

The Internet is the basis of hardware, software and data and the connections that join it all together. It consists of millions of computers – of all shapes and sizes – in tens of thousands of computer networks, throughout the world. They are joined through a mixture of special high-speed cables, microwave links and ordinary public and private telephone lines.

The World Wide Web is one of the ways of organising and looking at the information held on the Internet. It is probably the most important way – and certainly the simplest – but there are others (see page 8).

What's in it for me?

If you have access to the Internet, you have access to:

◆ **400+ million host computers**. These are the ones that provide services and information, any of which could be useful to you in your work, your travelling, your academic research or your hobbies.

◆ **Over 1 billion people.** You will already know of friends and relations who are on the Internet, and you will probably discover more once you start using it – and you could find new friends, customers, fellow enthusiasts, problem-solvers.

◆ **Terabytes (thousands of gigabytes) of files** containing programs – including the software that you need for working on the Internet – books, articles, pictures, video, sounds and much else.

◆ **A whole raft of services**, such as financial advice, banking, stock market information and trading, airline and train times and reservations, news and weather reports, small-ads and electronic shopping malls.

Who owns the Net?

The computers, networks and connections that make up the Internet are owned and run by thousands of separate businesses, government agencies, universities and individuals but no-one owns the Internet as a whole.

Take note

There will be even more computers and people on-line by the time you read this! The Internet has grown at a phenomenal rate – if the number of users continues to grow at its current rate, everyone in the World will be online in about five years. I don't quite think so...

The World Wide Web

This is the fastest-growing aspect of the Internet. It consists of billions of pages, held in millions of computers, joined together by *hypertext* links and viewed through a *web browser*, such as Internet Explorer (Chapter 2). The links allow you to jump from one page to another, which may be on the same machine or on one far, far away. The sheer number of pages, and the fact that millions are added or changed every day, mean that there can be no comprehensive index to the Web, but there are *directories* and *search engines* (Chapter 4) to help you to find what you want.

Some pages are simple text, but most are illustrated with graphics. Some have video or sound clips that you can enjoy on-line; other have links to files – programs, documents, pictures or multimedia clips – that you can *download* into your computer. Some pages work interactively, or act as places where people can meet and 'chat' by typing or talking.

Take note

Words in *bold italics* are in the Jargon on page 9.

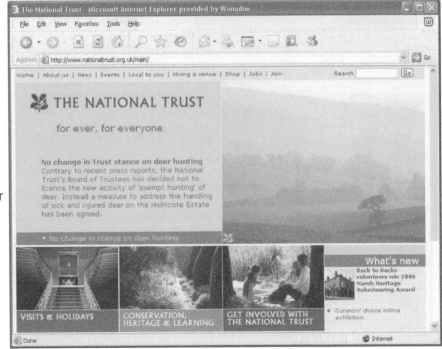

The old meets the new. The National Trust runs one of the most popular web sites in the UK, with thousands of visitors every day.

Electronic mail

These are messages sent to other individuals on the Internet. Think of them more like memos than postal mail. A message can be easily copied to other users; and when you receive an incoming message, you can attach your reply to it, or forward it on to a third party. You can also attach documents and graphics files to messages (see *Files by mail*, page 86).

The mail will sometimes get through almost instantaneously, but at worst it will be there within a few hours. The delay is because not all of the computers that handle mail are constantly in touch with each other. Instead, they will **log on** at regular intervals to deal with the mail and other services.

Key points about e-mail:

- E-mail is **fast**, **cheap** and (generally) very **reliable**.

- Every service provider offers **e-mail** access.

- As with **snail mail**, to send someone e-mail you need their address, and the best way to get that is to ask them.

Take note

E-mail software, such as Outlook Express, can be run off-line, and this is an good way to handle your mail if you use a dial-up connection. Go on-line to collect any new mail and to send any messages that you have written, then hang up the phone, read your mail and write your replies and new messages at your leisure, without clocking up phone charges.

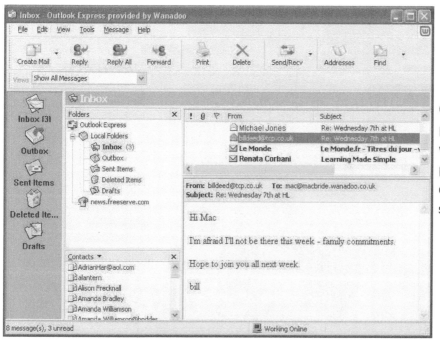

Outlook Express is probably the most widely-used e-mail program – and it's certainly one of the simplest to use.

WWW URLs

Don't you just love TLAs (Three Letter Acronyms)? The Internet is full of them. A **WWW URL** is a World Wide Web Uniform Resource Locator and it gives the location of a page.

Every computer site that is linked to the Internet has its own unique address, also referred to as a *domain name*. This is made up of two or more names, separated by dots, e.g.:

www.virgin.co.uk

The central part of the address identifies the organisation, which is usually derived from its name.

The other parts of the address follow certain conventions.

At the right-hand end there will be the country code, though this is omitted for US-based and international organisations. Examples are:

au	Australia	ca	Canada	de	Germany
es	Spain	fi	Finland	fr	France
hk	Hong Kong	ie	Ireland	it	Italy
jp	Japan	nz	New Zealand	uk	UK

The next part of the address, working from the right, identifies the nature of the organisation. The most common ones are:

com	commercial	(USA and international)
co	commercial	(outside the USA)
edu	educational	(USA)
ac	academic	(outside the USA)
net	network provider	
gov	government department	
org	non-commercial organization	

On the left-hand side there may be one or more other names to identify a computer, or part of a computer, within the site. These are variable, as they can be set by the organisation. Some common ones are:

www	the organisation's Web site
mail	the organisation's e-mail site
search	a search facility at the site

Take note

All domain names (site addresses) must be registered with InterNIC, the controlling body, to make sure that each is unique. If you want a domain name for your business (or personal) site, talk to your access provider.

Some typical examples are:

    micros.hensa.ac.uk

The computer on which the *micros* files are stored, at the University of Lancaster (*hensa*), an *ac*ademic site in the *UK*.

    sunsite.unc.edu

This is a *site* sponsored by *Sun* computers, within the University of North Carolina, an *edu*cational organisation in the USA.

    www.tcp.co.uk
    mail.tcp.co.uk

The Web site and e-mail server of my provider, *TCP* (Total Connectivity Providers), a *com*mercial organisation in the *UK*.

Web pages

A web page URL may be a simple name:

    http://www.cnet.com

This is the top page of the *cnet* site. *http://* identifies it as a WWW URL. *www* is how web addresses usually start.

Many can be recognised by their *html* or *htm* endings, which shows that they are hypertext pages.

    http://www.boutell.com/newfaq/privacy/worm.html

This page is about *worm* viruses, in the new frequently asked questions (*newfaq*) folder at *Boutell*'s web (*www*) site.

Some URLs are more complex:

    http://www.bbc.co.uk/bbc7/listenagain/thursday/

This takes us to the *thursday* area in the */bbc7/listenagain/ thursday* directory at *www.bbc.co.uk*.

On some sites, web pages are generated as they are needed by a program which draws on a database of information. For example, this URL takes you to a book's page at Amazon.

http://www.amazon.co.uk/exec/obidos/ASIN/0750653396/qid=
    1149848495/sr=1-5/ref=sr_1_3_5/203-6898864-2727126

E-mail addresses

The standard pattern for a person's e-mail address is:

    name@provider

However, there are quite a few variations to the basic pattern. For example, this is my address at TCP (Total Connectivity Providers), my local provider, where they follow the standard pattern:

    macbride@tcp.co.uk

TCP are small enough that most of their members can choose their names without restriction. At organisations with millions of members, such as AOL, Hotmail or Yahoo! mail, you may have to tack on a number to make a name unique, e.g.

    macbride252@yahoo.co.uk

For business users, the address is built from the domain name of the firm, and the person's real name or initials, e.g. if John Smith joined our publishers, his address would be:

    john.smith@elsevier.co.uk

For home users on broadband, where several people may share the connection, the address includes what looks like a domain name, as well as the personal name of each user, e.g.

    mac@macbride.fs.net

Tip

E-mail addresses are hard to guess and there are no proper directories. If you want someone's address, the simplest way to get it is to phone and ask them to send an e-mail to you. Every message carries its sender's address.

Take note

It is easy to mistype an e-mail address, but you should only have to type it once for each person. Every mail system has an Address Book file where you can store addresses (see page 90).

Other uses of the Net

Newsgroups and mailing lists

They are a combination of bulletin boards and newsletters, each dedicated to a specific interest, topic, hobby, profession or obsession. At the last count there were over 70,000 different newsgroups, plus a smaller set of mailing lists.

◆ A mailing list is a direct extension of e-mail. Messages to the list are sent individually to the list's subscribers – and subscription is normally free and open to all.

◆ Newsgroups are more centralised. The messages – here called articles – are initially sent to the computer that hosts the group. News servers collect new articles from the groups several times a day and hold them in store. If you want to read the news, you connect to your *news server* and download articles from there.

FTP

FTP – File Transfer Protocol – is the standard method for copying files across the Internet. FTP *host computers* hold archives, open to anyone to search and *download* files from. Some hosts have directories into which you can *upload* files, for others to share. You can download files through a web browser, but to upload you normally need a dedicated FTP program.

FTP URLs always specify the path from the top to the directory containing the file. The filename is the last item on the list.

ftp://ftp.temple.edu/pub/info/funstuff/smiley

This is the address of the file *smiley*, which will tell you all you want to know – and probably a lot that you don't – about the *smileys* (page 100) that are sometimes used in e-mail and newsgroup messages. It is in the *funstuff* directory, inside the *info* directory, in the *pub* directory of the *ftp* computer at *Temple* University in the USA.

Take note

E-mail and newsgroups work in similar ways and can be handled by the same software. Outlook Express is the mail and news software supplied with Internet Explorer.

Access provider – an organisation offering access to some or all of the services available over the Internet.

ASCII – the American Standard Code for Information Interchange. The ASCII code is a set of characters – letters, digits and symbols. ASCII text is plain, unformatted text.

Bandwidth – strictly refers to the capacity of the phone line, but is also used to refer to other net resources. If someone refers to your e-mail or your web site as being a 'waste of bandwidth', they didn't think much of it!

Binary files – any that are not plain ASCII text, e.g. images, programs and formatted text from word-processors.

Browsing – moving from one site to another on the World Wide Web, enjoying the scenery and following up interesting leads.

Byte – the basic unit of data. One byte can hold one character or a number from 0 to 255. A byte is made up of 8 **bits**, each of which can be 0 or 1, or an on/off electrical signal.

Content provider – organisation providing information and/or services to web users.

Dial-up connection – the method used by some home users, where you get on-line to the Internet by dialling your access provider. Many home users and most organisations now get on-line through broadband, giving an always-on, high-speed connection.

Directory – web site holding an organised set of links (thousands of them!). The better ones only have links to reviewed and selected sites.

Download – copy a file from the Internet to your own computer.

FAQs (Frequently Asked Questions) – at most places on the Internet where you can ask for help, you will find a FAQ list – a set of common questions, and their answers. Check the FAQs first, before asking a question.

FTP – File Transfer Protocol – a way of copying files across the Internet. FTP *host computers* hold archives, open to anyone to search and *download* files from. Some hosts have directories into which you can *upload* files, for others to share. You can download files through a web browser, but to upload you normally need a dedicated FTP program.

Freeware – free software! Some of it is excellent. The Net has a long tradition of sharing.

Gigabyte – a thousand megabytes or 1,000,000,000 bytes. This is the equivalent of around 2000 thick paperback books.

Gigahertz (Ghz) – 1000 Mhz, or 1,000,000,000 cycles a second (see *Megahertz*).

Home page – on a web site, the home page is the top one of a set, or a user's only published page. On a browser, the home page is the one that the browser will go to when it first starts.

Host computer – one that provides a service for Internet users. The service may be simple pages of information, access to files for downloading, a place to meet and chat with other users, or a complex interactive service.

Hypertext – documents linked so that clicking on a button, icon or keyword takes you into the related document – wherever it may be. Web pages are written in **HTML** (HyperText Markup Language) which handles links in a standardised way.

ISP (Internet Service Provider) – alternative name for Access Provider.

LAN (Local Area Network) – network operating within one site or organisation.

Log on – connect to a network or the Internet. This gives grammar purists a headache. As a noun, 'logon' – the act of connection – is one word. So, to match, the verb should be one word, but that gives 'logonned' and 'logonning' (aargh!!) instead of 'logged on' and 'logging on'. Just to make life really interesting, some people talk of 'log *in*'. Don't let it get to you.

Megahertz (Mhz) – 1,000,000 times a second. Processor speed, and other electronic functions are measured in hertz.

Modem – (**mo**dulator-**dem**odulator) a device which translates digital computer signals into an analogue form for transmission down the ordinary phone lines.

Network – a set of linked computers. On a LAN, users can share printers and networked resources. On any network – including the Internet – users can communicate and share data with each other.

Newbie – someone new to the Internet. Just remember, everybody was a newbie once.

News server – a computer at an Internet access provider's site that collects newsgroup articles for the benefit of its users.

Off-line – using your e-mail software or browser while not connected to the Internet. Mail can be read or written offline.

On-line – connected to the Internet (and clocking up phone charges!).

Portal – an Internet site which offers a range of services, including organised links into the Web. Portals aim to encourage as many users as possible to come through their site on their way into the Internet – and to read the adverts that pay for it all!

Search engines – web sites that hold searchable indexes to web pages and other Internet resources.

Shareware – software that you can try for free, but for which you should pay a (small) fee to continue to use.

Site – set of web pages run by one individual or organisation. The site may occupy one or more computers all by itself, or be one of many in a shared space.

Smiley – used mainly in e-mail, smileys are cartoon faces created from symbols and letters, e.g. :-)

Surfing – same as *browsing*.

Terabyte – 1000 *gigabytes*.

Upload – copy a file from your computer onto an Internet host computer.

Web browser – program that lets you leap between hypertext links to read text, view graphics and videos, and hear sounds. The leading browser is Internet Explorer.

2 Internet Explorer

The IE display

To view the World Wide Web you need a browser, and Internet Explorer (IE) is the one supplied with Windows. At the time of writing we are on version 6.0, but any version from 4.0 onwards has much the same features.

The main part of the window is used for the display of Web pages. Above this are the control elements. The **Menu bar** contains the full command set, with the most commonly used ones duplicated in the **Standard Toolbar**.

◆ The **Address** shows you where you are. You can type an URL (page 5) here to open a page. Up to 20 URLs are stored and can be selected from here, for easy revisiting.

◆ The **Links** offer an easy way to connect to selected places. Initially, they connect to pages on Microsoft's site, but you can replace them or add your own.

The Toolbars can be turned on or off as needed, but if you want the maximum viewing area click the **Fullscreen** icon.

The **Explorer Bar** can be opened to search the Internet (page 52), or use the Favorites (page 34) or History (page 38).

The **Status Bar** shows how much of an incoming file has been loaded. This can also be turned off if you don't want it.

The Standard toolbar

■ **Navigation tools**

 Previous page

 Next page (if loaded)

 Stop loading

 Reload page

Go to your Home page (page 14)

■ **Open in Explorer Bar**

 Search the Internet

Favorites folder

 History folder

■ **Other tools**

 Toggle Fullscreen mode on/off

 Start your mail/ news software

Print the page

Basic steps

- **Display options**

1 Click on **View**.

2 Point to **Toolbars** and turn them on (✓) or off from the submenu.

3 Click on **Status Bar** to turn it on or off.

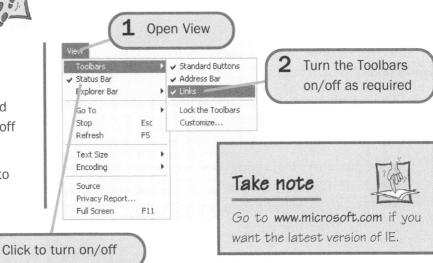

1 Open View

View		
Toolbars ▶	✓ Standard Buttons	
✓ Status Bar	✓ Address Bar	
Explorer Bar ▶	✓ Links	
Go To ▶	Lock the Toolbars	
Stop Esc	Customize...	
Refresh F5		
Text Size ▶		
Encoding ▶		
Source		
Privacy Report...		
Full Screen F11		

2 Turn the Toolbars on/off as required

3 Click to turn on/off

Take note

Go to **www.microsoft.com** if you want the latest version of IE.

Menu bar

Title of current page

Drag here to resize or move a toolbar

Links buttons

Standard toolbar

Address

Explorer bar

Status bar

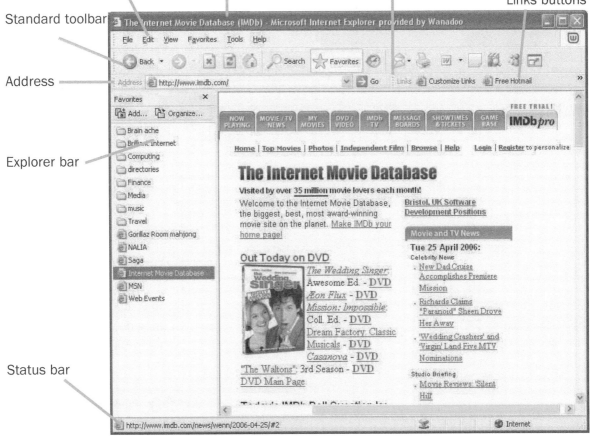

General options

The Internet Options control many aspects of Explorer's display and of how it works. Start on the **General** tab.

◆ Choose your **Home page**. This can be left blank or you can always start your browsing at the same place (e.g. a directory such as Yahoo! - see page 30).

◆ Set the disk space for storing files of visited pages. When you revisit, Explorer will use these and only download new files if the pages have changed - allocate lots of space for faster browsing.

◆ Set the **Accessibility** options and choose your own **Colors** and **Fonts** for maximum visibility, if needed.

1 Open the **Tools** menu and select **Internet Options...**

2 Go to **General**.

3 For the **Home page**, type the URL (or click **Use Current** if you are on that page), or click **Use Blank**.

4 Click **Settings**.

5 Select when to **check for new versions of stored pages** – Every visit is usually best.

6 Set the amount of space for storage.

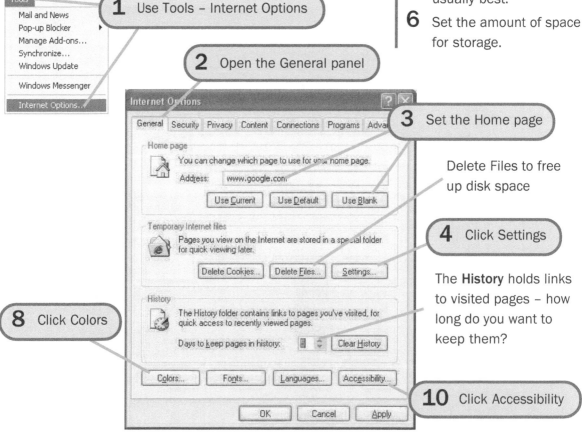

1 Use Tools – Internet Options

2 Open the General panel

3 Set the Home page

Delete Files to free up disk space

4 Click Settings

The **History** holds links to visited pages – how long do you want to keep them?

8 Click Colors

10 Click Accessibility

14

7 Click **OK**.

❑ **High visibility**

8 Click [Colors...].

9 Set the colours for high contrast and click **OK**. Set **Fonts** in the same way.

10 Click [Accessibility...].

11 Set Explorer to ignore the pages' own colours and fonts – so that yours are used instead.

12 Click [OK].

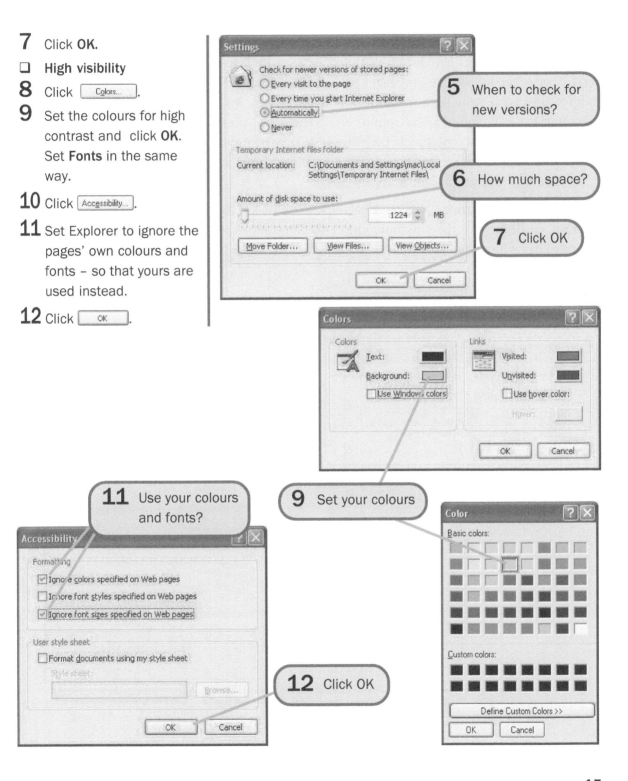

5 When to check for new versions?

6 How much space?

7 Click OK

9 Set your colours

11 Use your colours and fonts?

12 Click OK

Security

Many web pages have **active content**, i.e. they contain multimedia files or applets (small applications) written in Java, ActiveX or other interactive languages. These should not be able to mess with your hard disks or access your data, but some hackers have found a way round the restrictions – and anti-virus software is not much help here. Active content makes browsing more interesting, and if you stick to major sites, should create no problems.

Initially the **Internet zone** (i.e. all web sites), should be set to **Medium** or **High**. Use the **Custom** option to fine-tune the settings later, when you have more experience.

1 Go to the **Security** tab.

2 Pick the **Internet zone**.

3 Select **Medium** or **High** security.

Or

4 Click [Custom Level...].

5 Tell Explorer how to deal with each type.

6 Click [OK].

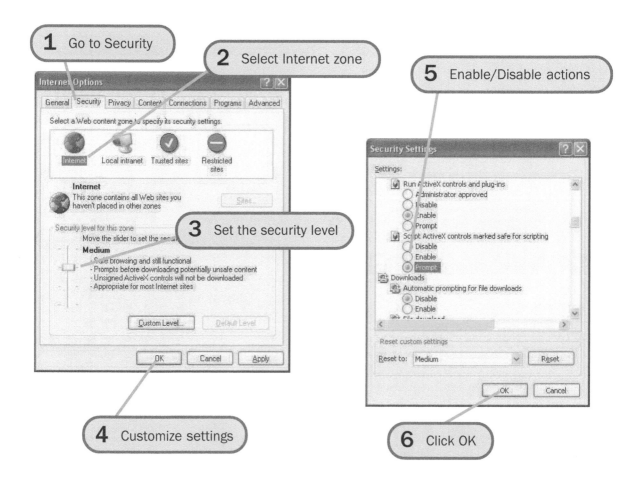

1 Go to Security

2 Select Internet zone

5 Enable/Disable actions

3 Set the security level

4 Customize settings

6 Click OK

Basic steps

1 Go to the **Security** tab.
2 Select a zone.
3 Click [Sites...].
4 Enter the site's URL and click .
5 Click [OK].

Building site lists

Some sites can be trusted more – and some far less – than others. With high security settings, active content will either not run at all or only do so after checking with you. If you can trust a site, low security settings will let you get the best out of its pages.

◆ The **Local intranet** has very low security. You should be able to trust anything that you find on your intranet, if you have one – but only if the organisation has clear policies and control over who can publish what.

◆ **Trusted sites** also have low security. If there are sites that you visit regularly which have a lot of active content, and which can be trusted, add them to this list.

◆ The **Restricted sites** have very high security. If there are sites that you want to visit, for their information or links, but where the active content is either instrusive or potentially dangerous, add them to this list.

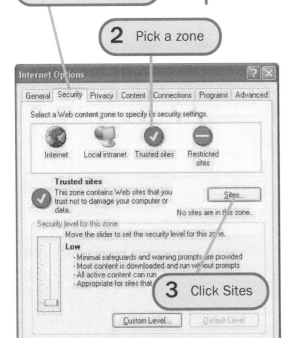

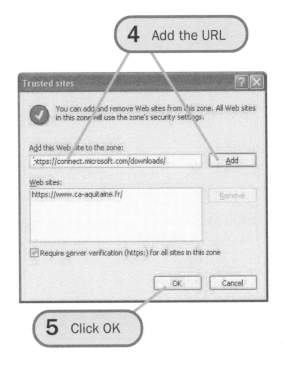

Programs

While you are surfing the Web with Internet Explorer, you may want to send an e-mail to someone – perhaps the person who runs a web site that interests you – or come across a link to a newsgroup, and want to read its articles. Explorer cannot handle mail and news, but it can link to other applications to do so and to handle other activities. The **Programs** tab is where you select the applications.

The choices that you are given depend upon what software is installed on your computer. The Windows XP and Explorer packages include:

◆ Outlook Express, for mail and news;

◆ NetMeeting, for instant Internet communications;

◆ Address Book, for Contacts list.

If you want an interactive Calendar, you need Microsoft Outlook or similar personal/group organiser software.

1 Open the **Internet Options** panel and go to the **Programs** tab.

2 Click the arrow beside each box and select the application.

3 Click [Apply].

1 Go to Programs

2 Select from the drop-down lists

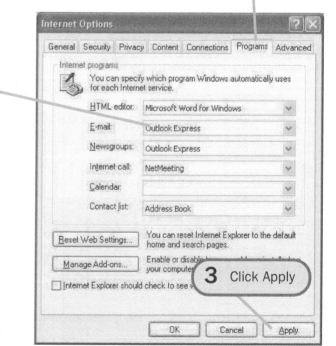

3 Click Apply

Tip

Don't click OK until you have finished setting the options on all the tabs – it closes the panel. Apply fixes your choices without closing the panel.

Multimedia options

1 Open the **Internet Options** panel and go to the **Advanced** tab.

2 Scroll down to the **Multimedia** section.

3 Click the options to turn them on or off as required.

4 Click [Apply] or [OK] to save and close the panel.

The Advanced tab contains loads of options, most of which should be left at their defaults until you have been surfing for a while. You will then have a better idea of how you want to handle them. However, there is one section that is worth dealing with now – multimedia. Pictures, audio and video files are sometimes essential, often merely decorative and always slow to load. Turn them off for faster browsing but pictures often contain links – if you can't see them, you may not be able to navigate some sites. You can turn them back on and reload a page to view the files, or simply click on a non-displayed image (it will appear as 🖾) to load it.

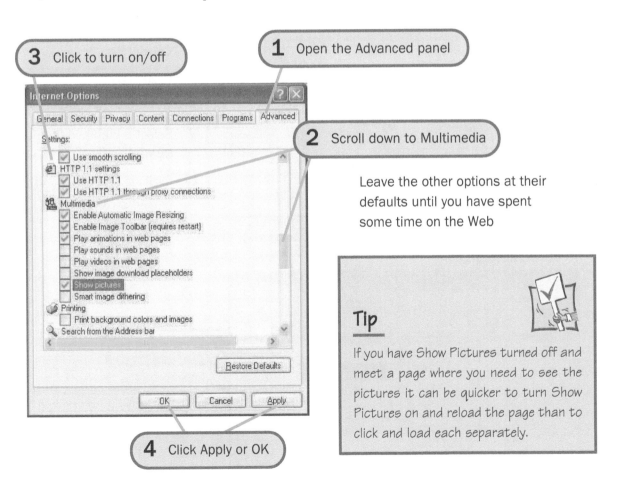

3 Click to turn on/off

1 Open the Advanced panel

2 Scroll down to Multimedia

Leave the other options at their defaults until you have spent some time on the Web

4 Click Apply or OK

Tip

If you have Show Pictures turned off and meet a page where you need to see the pictures it can be quicker to turn Show Pictures on and reload the page than to click and load each separately.

Customize the toolbars

The Standard toolbar initially has a dozen buttons, but there another dozen available for you to choose from – and you can remove any buttons that you do not use.

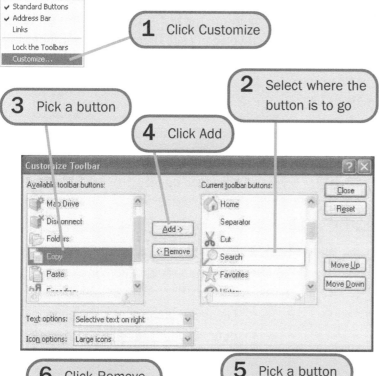

Basic steps

1 Right-click on the toolbar and select **Customize...** from the context menu.

- **To add a button**

2 Select a button in the **Current** list – the new one will be added above (to the left of) this.

3 Select the button to add.

4 Click [Add ->].

- **To remove a button**

5 Select the button in the **Current** list.

6 Click [<- Remove].

- **To rearrange buttons**

7 Select a button in the **Current** list.

8 Click [Move Up] or [Move Down] to change its position.

Basic steps

1 Right-click on the toolbar and select **Customize...** from the context menu.

- **Text options**

2 At the **Customize Toolbar** dialog box, click the arrow to open the **Text options** list.

3 Select an option.

- **Icon options**

4 In the **Icon options** list, select **Large** or **Small**.

5 Click [Close].

Button appearance options

You can adjust the appearance of the buttons in two ways:

◆ Text labels can be displayed on all buttons, on selected ones or on none. Labels can be useful at first, but removing them leaves room for more buttons on the toolbar, which you may find more useful later.

◆ You can have large or small icons – though note that this does not work on some screen displays. Try it on yours.

5 Click Close

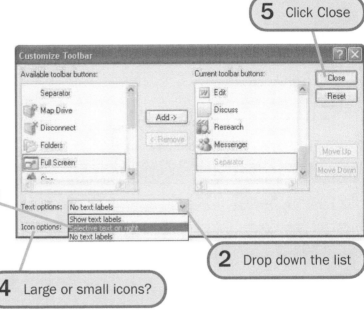

3 Pick an option

2 Drop down the list

4 Large or small icons?

Tip

If, after adding and removing buttons, you decide that you don't like the way things are, click [Reset] to put it back to normal – and start to customize the toolbar again from scratch.

Show text labels

Select text on right

No text labels

Getting Help

If you need more Help on any aspect of Internet Explorer, check its Help pages - pretty well everything is covered, though possibly in more detail than you might want!

There are basically three ways to find Help: browse through the contents, use the index or search for key words.

■ **To browse for Help**

1 Open the **Help** menu and select **Contents and Index**.

2 Switch to the **Content** tab, if it is not on top.

3 Click 📖 to open a 'book' of topics.

4 Click 📄 to display a Help page.

5 On a Help page, click ⊞ for more on a subtopic.

6 Click Related Topics then click on a title to go to a related page.

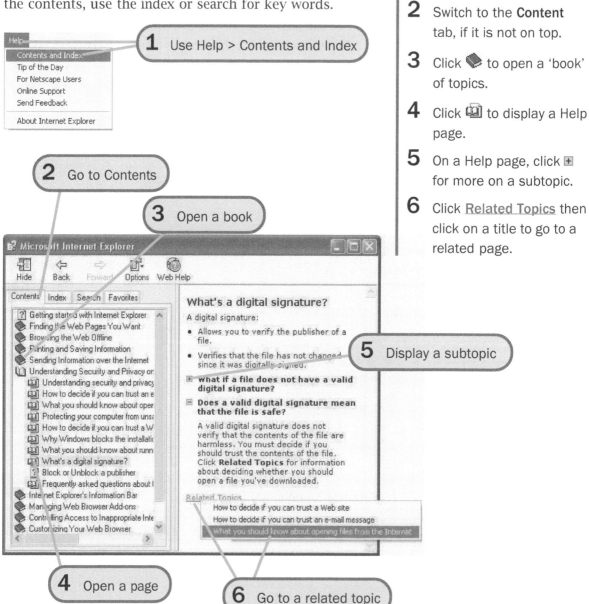

1 Use Help > Contents and Index

2 Go to Contents

3 Open a book

4 Open a page

5 Display a subtopic

6 Go to a related topic

Basic steps

■ **To use the Index**

1 Open the **Help** menu and select **Contents and Index**.

2 Switch to the **Index** tab.

3 Start to type a word to describe what you are looking for.

4 Select an entry from the list and click [Display].

5 You may be offered a set of topics – select one and click [Display].

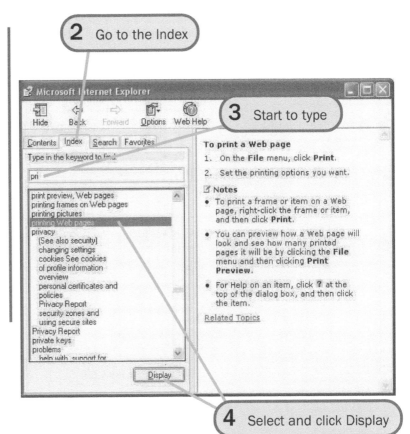

2 Go to the Index

3 Start to type

4 Select and click Display

Tip

If you find a Help page that you think you might want to refer to again, go to the Favorites tab and add it to your Favorites. You can jump straight back to it next time you want it.

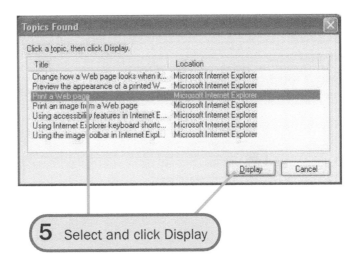

5 Select and click Display

Searching for help

If you are clear and specific in defining your key words, a search can be the quickest way to find the Help you want.

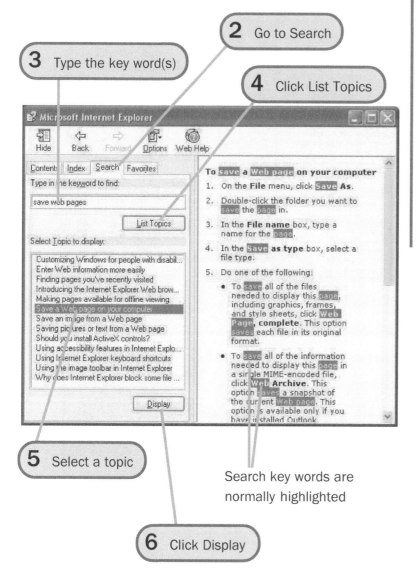

3 Type the key word(s)

2 Go to Search

4 Click List Topics

5 Select a topic

Search key words are normally highlighted

6 Click Display

1 Open the **Help** menu and select **Contents and Index**.

2 Switch to the **Search** tab.

3 Type one or more words to describe what you are looking for.

4 Click [List Topics].

5 Select an entry from the list.

6 Click [Display].

Take note

Your search key words are normally highlighted in the Help page displays. This can be useful, especially when you are looking for less common topics as it will direct you to the relevant part of the page. On the other hand, the highlighting can make the text harder to read. With this in mind, IE gives you the option of turning the highlight off – see opposite.

Help page options

- **Printing Help pages**

1 Select the Help page.

2 If you only want to print part of a page, select it first.

3 Click the Options button and select **Print...**

4 To print part of a page, click **Print the selected heading ...**

Or

5 To print it all, choose **Print the selected topic**.

6 Click [OK].

7 At the **Print** dialog box, set the options for your printer as appropriate.

The Options drop-down list in the Help page toolbar has a short set of commands that you can use while working in the Help system. Most of them are also present as toolbar buttons. They are all very straightforward, with the possible exception of Print. We'll have a closer look at that.

Hides the tabs display (and is then replaced by Show which displays them)

Back to previous Help page viewed

Forward again (after going Back)

Go to Microsoft's site for Help

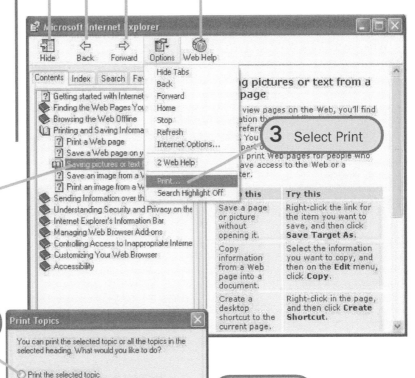

1 Select the page

3 Select Print

5 Print the whole page

4 Print the selected part of the page

6 Click OK

Exercises

1 Start up and log on to your PC, if necessary.

2 Run Internet Explorer. Identify the screen elements shown on pages 12 and 13. Do you have any toolbar buttons not shown there? You may have, as installations vary. If you do, find out what they are for. Pause the cursor over a button to see its name, then look it up in the Help system.

3 Work through the Internet Options to suit your way of working. In particular, set the home page, history and the screen colours.

4 Go to the Help system and use the Index or Search modes to find out about the Information bar. What is it and what is it used for?

5 Use the Help system to find out about the pop-up blocker. Why might you want to turn this on?

3 Navigating the Web

Hypertext links

The World Wide Web is held together by millions of hypertext links. These may take you from one page to another within a site or off to a far-distant site – though some pages are dead-ends, which is when the Back button comes in handy!

The links may be underlined words embedded in the text or presented as a list, or may be built into pictures. They are always easy to spot. When you point to a link, the cursor changes to ⌐⟨ᕼᒣ⟩ and the Status line shows the address of the linked page.

- Web pages often have links to other pages (in the site or elsewhere) on the same topic, which may lead on to others. Once you have started you can browse the links – the trick is to find a good place to start...

Hypertext links are usually underlined and coloured blue

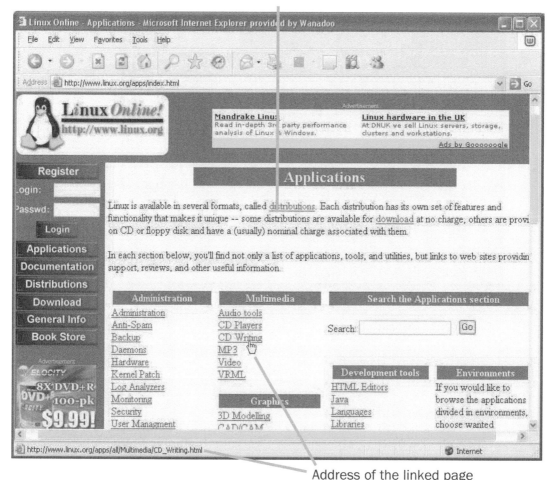

Address of the linked page

Interactive pages

Tip

If it is not obvious how a page is linked, move the mouse slowly over it, looking for the hand pointer and for addresses in the Status bar.

Many pages now have interactive menus, written in Java, ASP or other web page programming languages. These vary, of course, but typically, when you point at an item on the main menu, a submenu opens up and clicking an entry here takes you to another page.

If you point at an interactive menu, you often get a pop-up label to tell you more about the option – you also normally get labels when you point at images

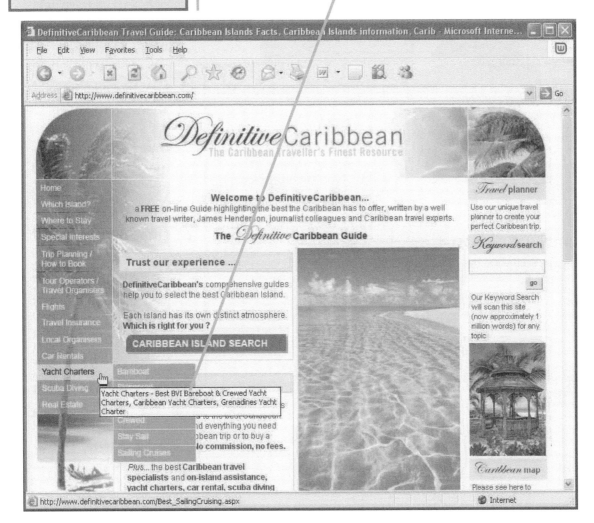

Starting to explore

The Internet is so big, where do you start browsing? A site such as Yahoo is probably as good a place as any. This offers a huge range of things to do and see within its own extensive system, but also has a massive directory of links to other sites.

If you know the address of a site, you can get there very easily. Yahoo! is at: **www.yahoo.com**.

To get there, we can type the address into the **Open** dialog box.

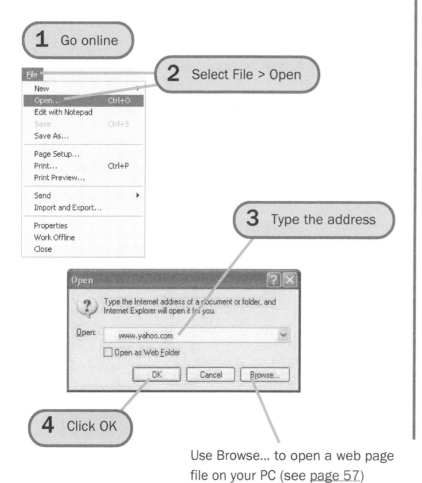

1 Go online

2 Select File > Open

File
New
Open...   Ctrl+O
Edit with Notepad
Save   Ctrl+S
Save As...

Page Setup...
Print...   Ctrl+P
Print Preview...

Send   ▶
Import and Export...

Properties
Work Offline
Close

3 Type the address

Open

? Type the Internet address of a document or folder, and Internet Explorer will open it for you.

Open: www.yahoo.com

☐ Open as Web Folder

OK   Cancel   Browse...

4 Click OK

Use Browse... to open a web page file on your PC (see page 57)

1 If you are not online, connect now.

2 Open the **File** menu and select **Open**.

3 Type in the address.

4 Click [OK].

5 The home page at Yahoo! has several different sets of links. The main set near the top are to areas within Yahoo! Click on a link to see what's there.

6 Links are easy to spot at Yahoo! If it's underlined, it's a link. Most images – especially the photos – are normally linked as well. Click on a link to go to the linked page.

7 Follow the links that interest you.

When you're ready to move on, click [◉ Back ▾] repeatedly until you reach the top page. We'll have a look at the Yahoo! directory next.

You can **search the Web** from here (page 50)

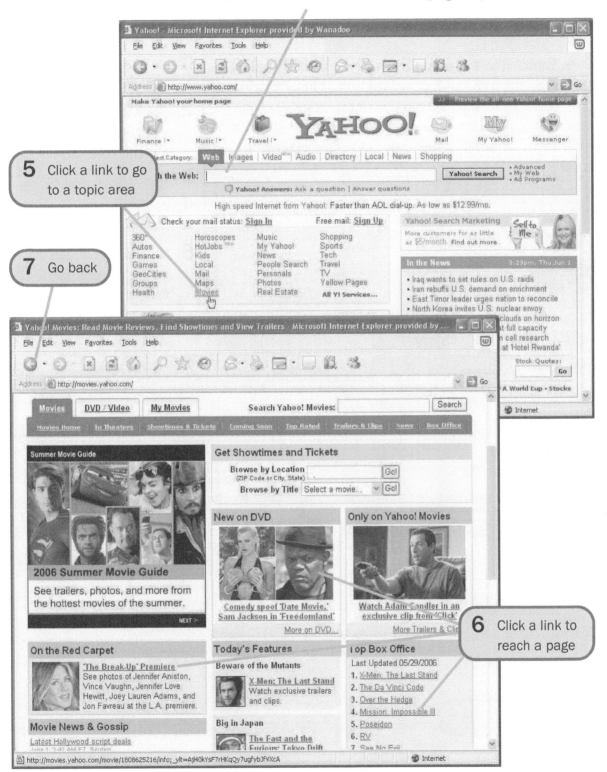

5 Click a link to go to a topic area

7 Go back

6 Click a link to reach a page

The Yahoo! directory

When Yahoo! first started it was simply a directory – though the best on the Web – with organised lists of links to selected sites. That directory is still there, and just as good as ever. The links are organised into a hierarchy of topics and subtopics of up to six levels or more. Take your time and explore it!

1 Go back to the opening page at Yahoo!

2 Scroll down to the **Web directory**, near the bottom of the page.

3 Click a topic heading.

4 At the next level, click on a subtopic heading.

5 Work down through the levels. You will start to find links to pages – click to go to the page.

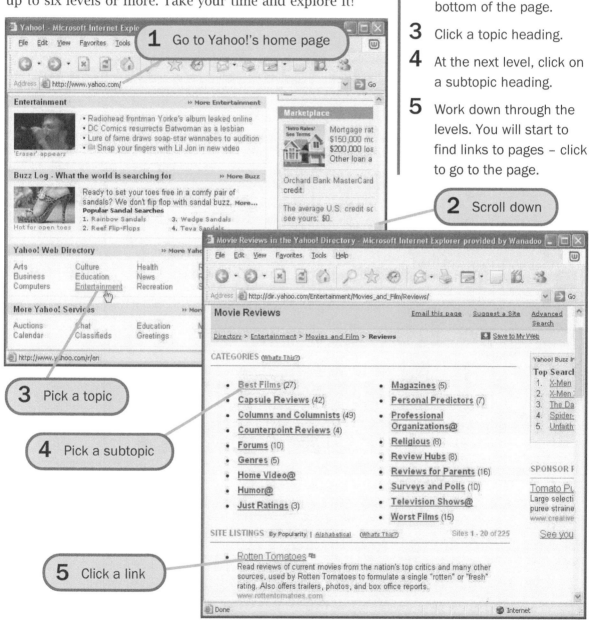

Basic steps

1 Click in the Address bar.

2 If an address is already present, it will be high-lighted – press [Delete] to delete it.

■ **To go to a new site**

3 Type the address and press [**Enter**].

■ **To revisit a site**

4 Click the arrow at the right of the bar and select an address from the drop-down list.

Or

5 Start to type the address.

6 If IE has been there recently, it will offer a list of possible addresses – click to use one.

Using the Address bar

You can type addresses directly into the Address bar, instead of using the Open dialog box – the result is exactly the same. But the Address bar is more than just a a place for entering addresses – it also stores them.

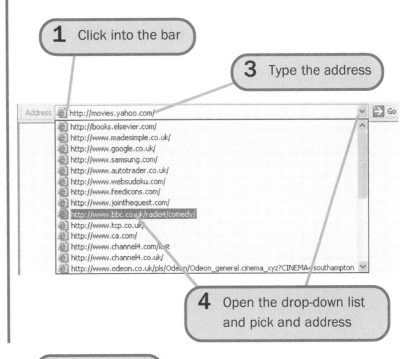

1 Click into the bar

3 Type the address

4 Open the drop-down list and pick and address

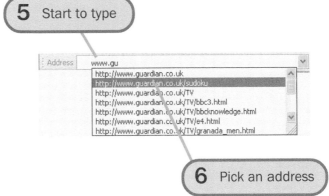

5 Start to type

6 Pick an address

Tip

You often see addresses written with **http://** at the start. You don't usually need to type this – the browser will assume that you want a Web address.

Favorites

Some good places are easy to find; others you discover after a long and painful search or by sheer chance. If you want to return to a page in future, add it to your Favorites. This stores the title and URL in a file and puts the title on the Favorites list.

◆ You must have the page open to be able to add it to the Favorites – but you can do this offline by opening the page from the History list (page 38).

◆ If the Favorites list is opened from the menu bar, it drops down the screen and closes after you have chosen.

◆ Using the toolbar button opens the Favorites in the Explorer bar, where it stays at hand until you choose to close it.

◆ You can store a Favorite in a folder as you create it.

■ **To revisit a Favorite**

1 Open **Favorites** and pick a page – you may need to open a submenu.

■ **To add pages to Favorites**

2 Open **Favorites**.

3 Select **Add to Favorites**.

4 Edit the title if necessary.

5 To add it to the main list, click ⌈ OK ⌋.

Or

6 To store it in a folder, click ⌈ Create in >> ⌋.

7 Select the folder.

8 Click ⌈ OK ⌋.

You can display the Favorites in the Explorer bar – click the star icon

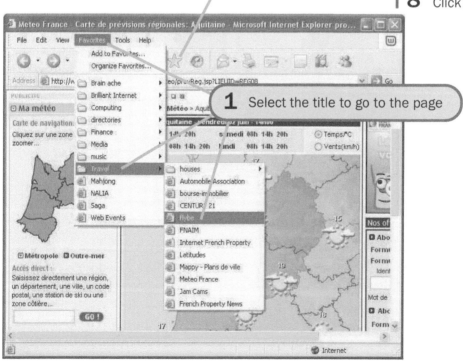

1 Select the title to go to the page

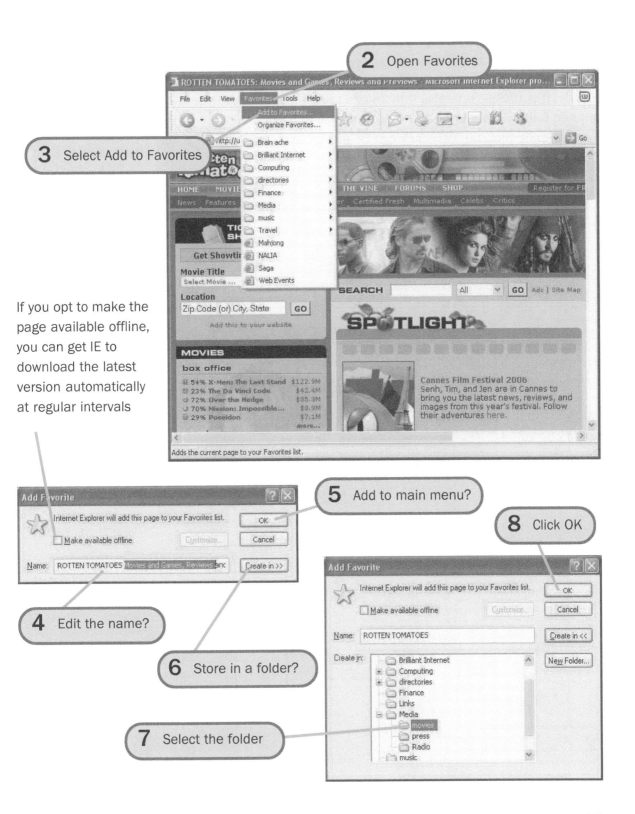

2 Open Favorites

3 Select Add to Favorites

If you opt to make the page available offline, you can get IE to download the latest version automatically at regular intervals

5 Add to main menu?

8 Click OK

4 Edit the name?

6 Store in a folder?

7 Select the folder

Organising Favorites

When your Favorites list gets so long that you can't find things quickly, it is time to organise it by moving related items into suitable folders. This is easily done. First you need to create some folders, then the Favorites can be moved in.

1 Click **Organize Favorites** on the **Favorites** menu or in the Explorer bar.

2 Click [Create Folder] and give the new folder a name.

3 To move a link into a folder, drag it over to the folder and drop it in.

Or

4 Select the link and click [Move to Folder...], then pick a folder from the list.

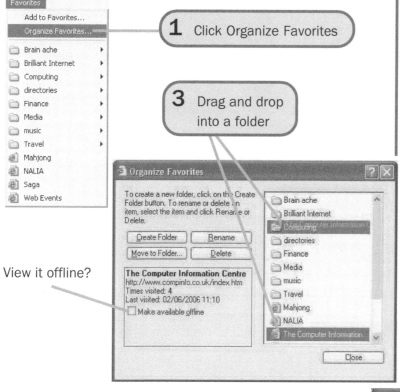

1 Click Organize Favorites

3 Drag and drop into a folder

View it offline?

2 Create a folder

4 Move using the dialog box

Desktop shortcuts

- **To create a shortcut**

1 Go to the page.

2 Drag the symbol from the Address bar onto the Desktop.

- **To use a shortcut**

3 Click on the icon to start IE and link to the page.

Do you use Desktop shortcuts to your most-used applications, or to documents that you want to reopen in a hurry? You can also create Desktop shortcuts to Internet sites. One click on the shortcut will then start the browser and make the connection.

1 Go to the page

2 Drag the icon onto the Desktop

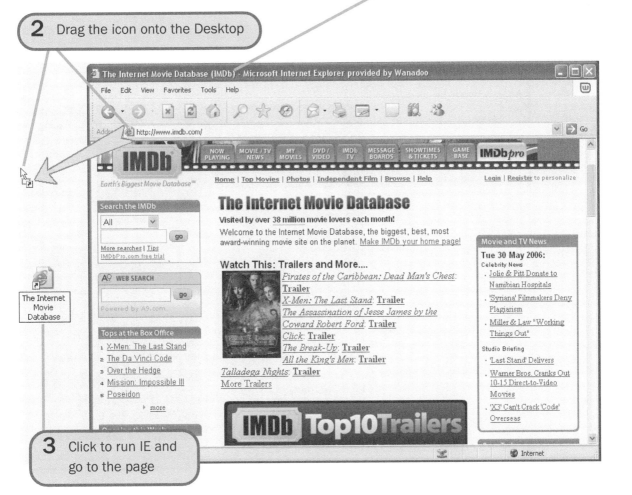

3 Click to run IE and go to the page

The History list

As you browse, each page is recorded in the History list as an Internet shortcut – i.e. a link to the page. Clicking the History button opens the list in the Explorer Bar, where the links are grouped into folders according to site or to when they were visited.

If you want to use the History after you have gone offline, open the **File** menu and turn on the **Work Offline** option. This may not work. You cannot open a page off-line if it draws information from its home site – whether to get fresh adverts or news updates, or because some of the page content is created actively while you view.

1 Click the **History** button to open the list in the Explorer Bar.

2 Click to open a site's folder.

3 Select the page.

4 Click the **X** at the top right of the Explorer Bar to close it.

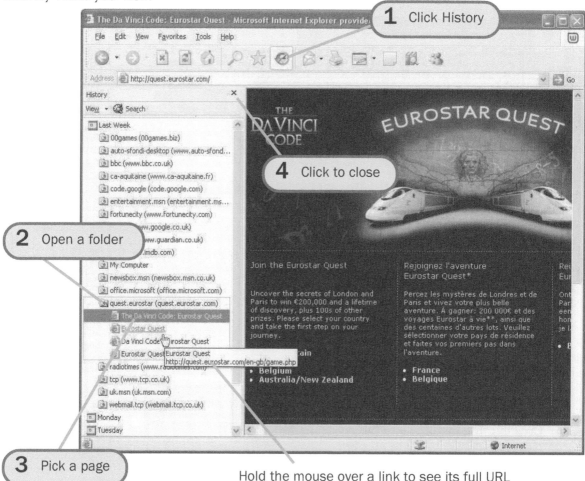

Hold the mouse over a link to see its full URL

Basic steps

To rearrange the list

1 Click the **View** button.

2 Select the order.

To delete items

3 Right-click on a page or folder name in the list.

4 Select **Delete** from the context menu.

Rewriting History

By Site is normally the best way to view the History list, but it can also be displayed grouped **By Date** or with individual pages listed **By Most Visited** or **By Order Visited Today**.

If it gets overcrowded, unwanted pages or sites can be deleted.

Tip

If you want to keep the current page at hand while you go to another, use File > New > Window to open a second window and use that to browse to other pages.

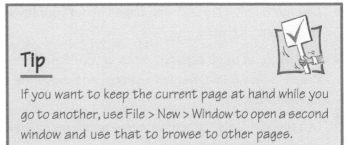

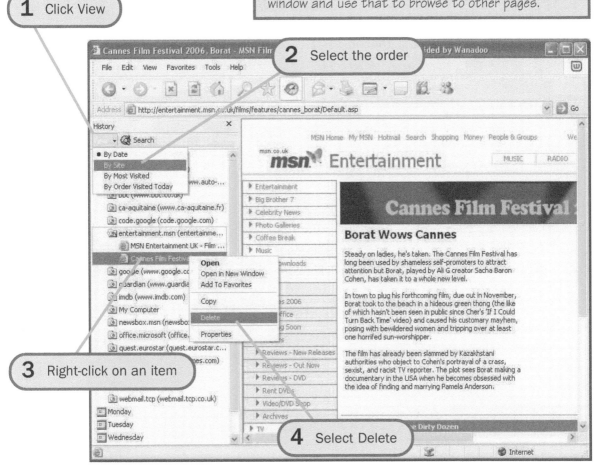

Exercises

1 Start Internet Explorer and go on-line, if necessary.

2 Go to Yahoo! at www.yahoo.com or uk.yahoo.com.

3 Identify at least three hyperlinked images and three text items – look for the hand pointer and check the content of the Status bar.

4 Use the Directory to find web pages about your favourite singer, actor or writer.

5 Add pages at three separate sites to your Favorites list. Create a new folder, called Research and move the new Favorites into it.

6 Use the History list to return to one of the first pages that you found in the Yahoo directory.

7 Create a Desktop shortcut to Yahoo!

4 Searching the Web

Search engines

You can find most things by browsing through directories such as Yahoo! (see page 30), but it can take a while – especially if you are researching an unusal topic. This is where the search engines come into play. At these sites you can search the Web for pages that meet your specifications.

Search engines vary in the way they collect and hold data, and in their degree of completeness – a 100% coverage is impossible as pages are added and changed constantly. If you don't find what you want at one, it is often worth trying another. The search techniques are similar at all the engines.

Simple searches

If you enter a single word, then – as you would expect – the engines will search for that word. If you enter two or more words, there are several possible responses:

◆ Most engines will search for pages that contain *any* of the words, but display first those those contain *all* of them, e.g. 'Beijing Peking' would find pages referring to the capital of China, however it was spelt. A search for 'graphics conversion software' would find all pages containing the word 'graphics', plus those containing 'conversion' and those with 'software' – and there will be millions. However, pages containing all three words – though not necessarily in that order, or related to each other – would be among the first results displayed.

◆ If the given words are enclosed in "double quotes", most engines will search only for that phrase. Look for "greenhouse effect" and you should find stuff on global warming, and not get pages on gardening!

Plurals and other endings

Some engines automatically truncate and extend words to cater for different possible endings. With these, a search for '**musi**cals' would also find 'music' and 'musicians'.

Take note

At a search engine, you do not actually search the Web, but you search their databases that hold key information about pages and sites on the Web – a direct search through those billions of pages would take far too long!

Advanced searches

These are much more varied than simple searches. Most support the use of logical operators.

Logical operators

Also known as Boolean operators, these can be used to link keywords. They are normally written in capitals.

AND   every word must match to produce a hit.

OR   any matching word will produce a hit

NOT   ignore pages containing this word.

If you use a mixture of operators, they will normally be evaluated in the order NOT, AND then OR, e.g.

boat AND sail OR yacht

will find pages with references to boats where sails are also mentioned, or to yachts.

boat AND sail OR paddle

will again find references to sailing boats, but will also pick up all 'paddle' pages - whether they relate to boats or not. This can be changed by putting round brackets () around the part you want to evaluate first. So, to find paddle boats or sail boats, you would need:

boat AND (sail OR paddle)

Include/exclude

Some engines will allow the use of the modifiers + (include) and - (exclude). Key words marked + must be present for a page to match; pages containing key words marked with - are to be ignored, e.g.

+"Tom Jones" Fielding –song

Should find pages about the book by Henry Fielding, but ignore the singer's fan clubs.

Google

Google is widely accepted as the best search engine. It has a phenomenally large database - over 15 billion pages at the time of writing - and is optimized for speed. The searches are fast - 1.3 million results in 0.14 of a second in the example overleaf - and the site is kept to the minimum, with no flashy graphics, adverts and other irrelevancies to slow things down.

To run a search at Google, type in one or more words to define what you are looking for, e.g, *classical harp sheet music*. The search engine will look first for sites that match all four words, then for those that match any two or any single word.

When it presents the results, they are in order of 'relevance', which is calculated in a complex, but effective way. This brings to the top of the result list those sites:

◆   that best match your words (because the words feature in the page's key words, title, headings and text);

◆   that other people have found to be the most valuable (as shown by the number of links to their pages and the number of visitors they get).

As a general rule, if you do not find good sites among the first 20 results of a Google search, it's because there aren't any out there, or because your search was badly defined. A single word will rarely be enough to focus a search properly - search for 'music' and you'll get nearly 3 billion results, covering every conceivable type. On the other hand, being too specific doesn't hurt, as Google seems to be able to pick out the words that matter. Look for 'Sandi Thom latest CD and pictures' and right there at the top of the results you will find several sites that can sell you just those things.

Tip

Google is where I always start searching and where I will usually find the links I need. As a general rule, if you can't find it through Google, it's not on the Web!

Basic steps

■ **Simple search**

1 Go to Google at
www.google.com

or

www.google.co.uk

2 Type one or more key
words.

3 Click [Search] or press
[Enter].

4 Click on a link.

Searching at Google

A simple search will generally do the job at Google – just type
in a few words to describe what you are looking for. Sometimes it helps to use its 'search within results' facility, which
allows you to focus in on a topic through two or more levels
of search.

Take note

If you are in the UK you can limit the
search to pages from the UK – click
the option under the search box.

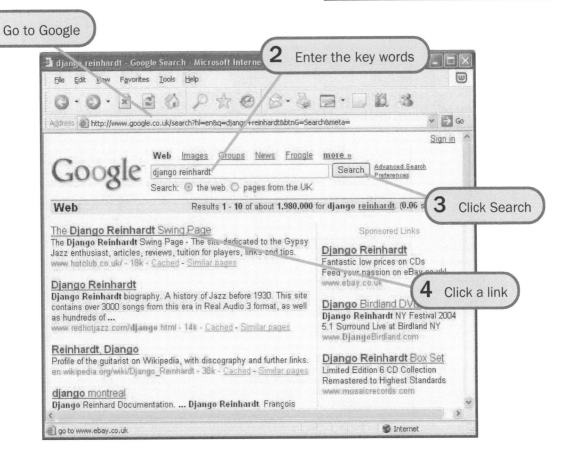

Searching within

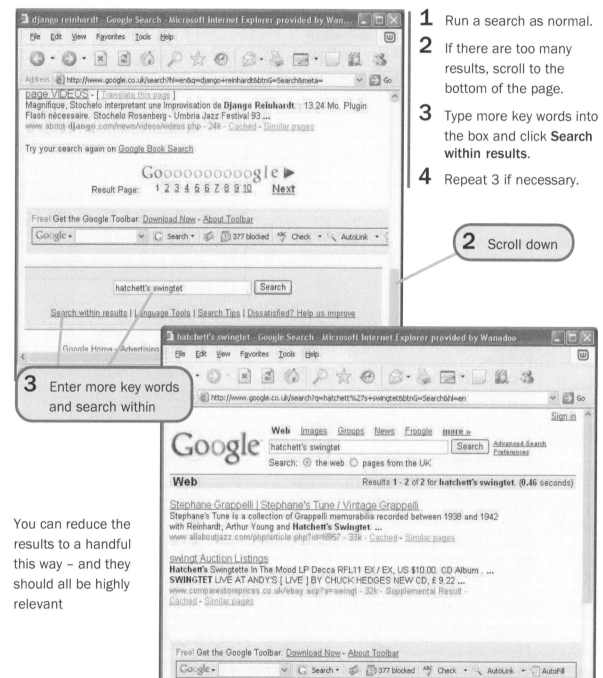

1 Run a search as normal.

2 If there are too many results, scroll to the bottom of the page.

3 Type more key words into the box and click **Search within results**.

4 Repeat 3 if necessary.

2 Scroll down

3 Enter more key words and search within

You can reduce the results to a handful this way – and they should all be highly relevant

Other search engines

There are several other search engines worth a visit, including these two.

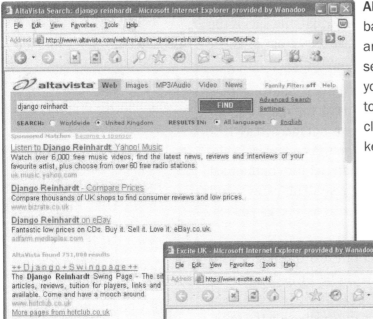

AltaVista (www.altavista.com) is a bare-bones search site, like Google, and equally fast and efficient. After searching the Web for something, you can click on the tabs along the top to find images, audio or video clips or news reports for the same key words.

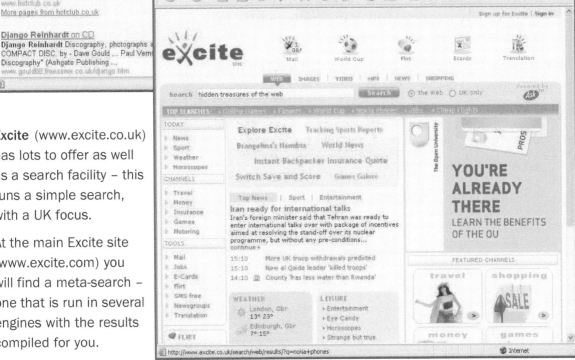

Excite (www.excite.co.uk) has lots to offer as well as a search facility – this runs a simple search, with a UK focus.

At the main Excite site (www.excite.com) you will find a meta-search – one that is run in several engines with the results compiled for you.

Advanced searches

Most advanced search routines follow the same pattern. Here's how you run one at Google.

If you go to the advanced search page, you can define a search more closely, specifying the type of file format, the age of the information, the language, and other aspects. Most of these options are quite straightforward; two are not:

◆ **Usage Rights** – there is a scheme for showing how people can use the material on a page, though fairly few sites take part. Just because a page is not marked as 'free to share' does not mean that it isn't. As a general rule, you cannot use other people's material for commercial purposes, but you can use it in student essays and similar things, and you can quote text as long as you say where it is from.

◆ **Safe Search** – Google can filter out text or images with explicit sex content. The filter can be turned on or off here, but the level of filtering – moderate or strict – is set on the Preferences page. Follow the link beside the inital Search box to set your preferences.

There are also topic-specific searches which allow you to hunt for information:

◆ in books or scholarly papers;

◆ about Apple, Unix, Linux or Microsoft systems;

◆ in US government sites;

◆ in US universities' web sites.

1 Go to Google.

2 Click the **Advanced Search** link beside the Search box.

3 Enter key words into the appropriate boxes.

4 Restrict the search by setting any or all options

■ the **Language**

■ the **File Format** to find PDF, postscript, Word, Excel, PowerPoint and rich text format files

■ the **Date**, to get only newer pages

■ **Occurrences** – whether to look in the title, text, URL or links to the page

■ the **Domain** – limit the search to one site, or to one country or type (e.g. .uk, .fr, .ac)

■ **Usage Rights** and **Safe Search** – see the main text.

5 Click [Google Search].

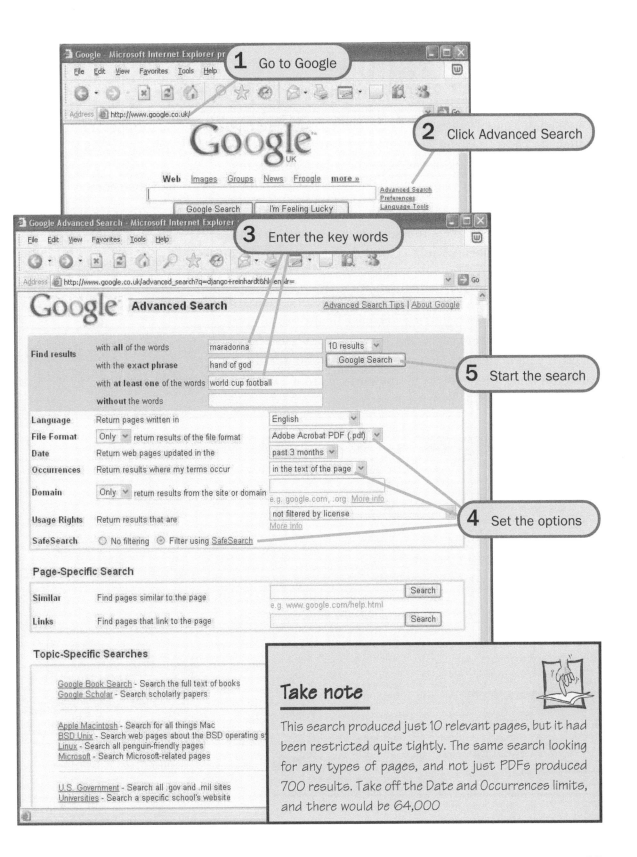

1 Go to Google

2 Click Advanced Search

3 Enter the key words

5 Start the search

4 Set the options

Take note

This search produced just 10 relevant pages, but it had been restricted quite tightly. The same search looking for any types of pages, and not just PDFs produced 700 results. Take off the Date and Occurrences limits, and there would be 64,000

49

Searching Yahoo!

We looked at Yahoo!'s directory in the last chapter. Browsing through its categories can be a good way to find stuff, but sometimes if you are looking for a specific topic, organisation, artist, program, or whatever, it can be quicker to search for it.

A simple search hunts through the whole Web, and will generally produce similar – though fewer – results than the same search at Google. You can search for images, video, audio, business, news and shopping.

You can restrict the search to the Yahoo! directory. This will produce far fewer results, but if a web page or site has an entry in the Yahoo! directory, it means that someone has visited, looked at it, and decided that it is worth including. You can search the whole directory, or if you start off from a category page, you can search just that category.

Basic steps

1 Go to Yahoo! at **www.yahoo.com**

Or

uk.yahoo.com

2 Enter your key words.

3 Select the search category – Web for a general search.

4 Click [Yahoo! Search].

5 Follow the links – the ones at the top and the right are to advertisers' sites.

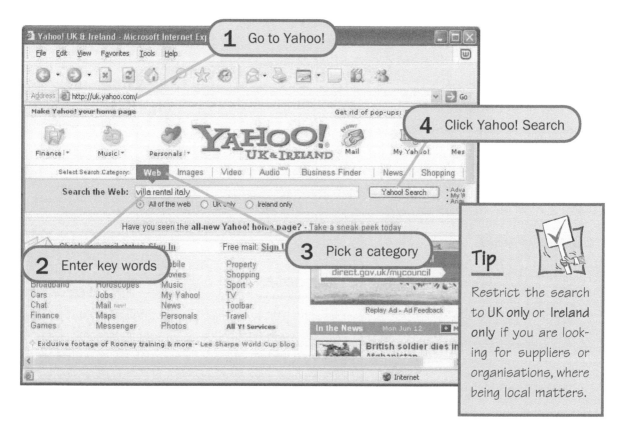

1 Go to Yahoo!

4 Click Yahoo! Search

2 Enter key words

3 Pick a category

Tip

Restrict the search to UK only or Ireland only if you are looking for suppliers or organisations, where being local matters.

50

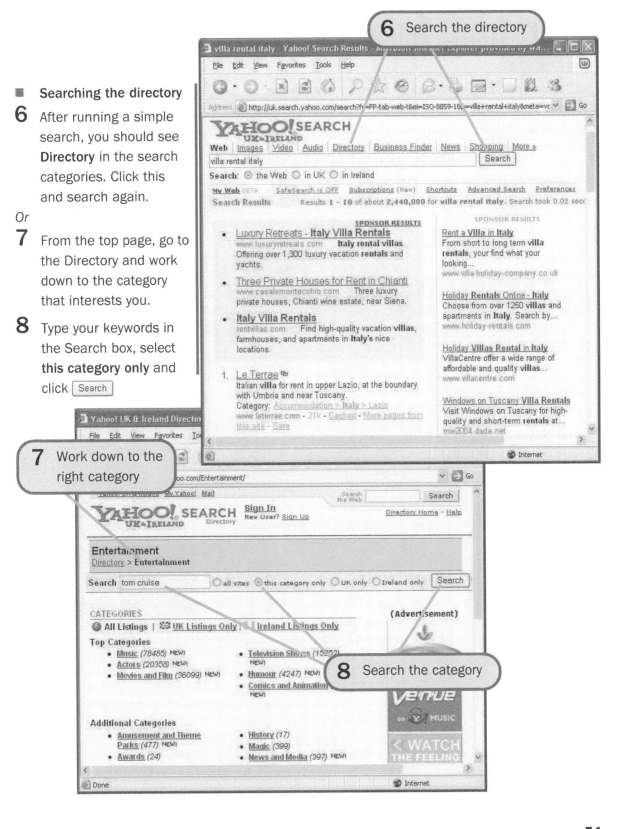

■ **Searching the directory**

6 After running a simple search, you should see **Directory** in the search categories. Click this and search again.

Or

7 From the top page, go to the Directory and work down to the category that interests you.

8 Type your keywords in the Search box, select **this category only** and click Search

6 Search the directory

7 Work down to the right category

8 Search the category

Searching from IE

You can run a search from within Internet Explorer using the Search option in the Explorer bar. The search will normally be performed by MSN search, though you can use other sites.

◆ The one big advantage of searches from the Explorer bar is convenience. The results stay visible while you visit the pages, so that you can quickly pick another page - or run another search.

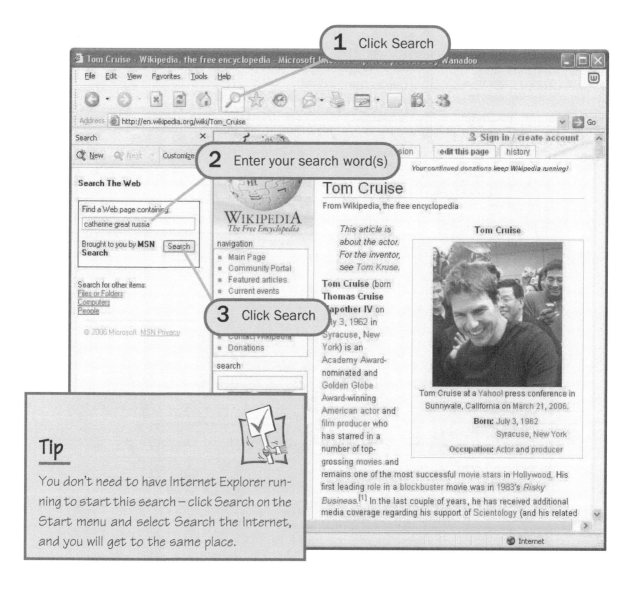

Tip

You don't need to have Internet Explorer running to start this search — click Search on the Start menu and select Search the Internet, and you will get to the same place.

5 Explore the other links.

6 If you don't find what you want, start a new search.

Or

7 Close the Explorer bar to free up the screen space.

Take note

One of the attractions of MSN search is that it offers previews of the pages that it finds, and these can help to identify which are most likely to be useful to you.

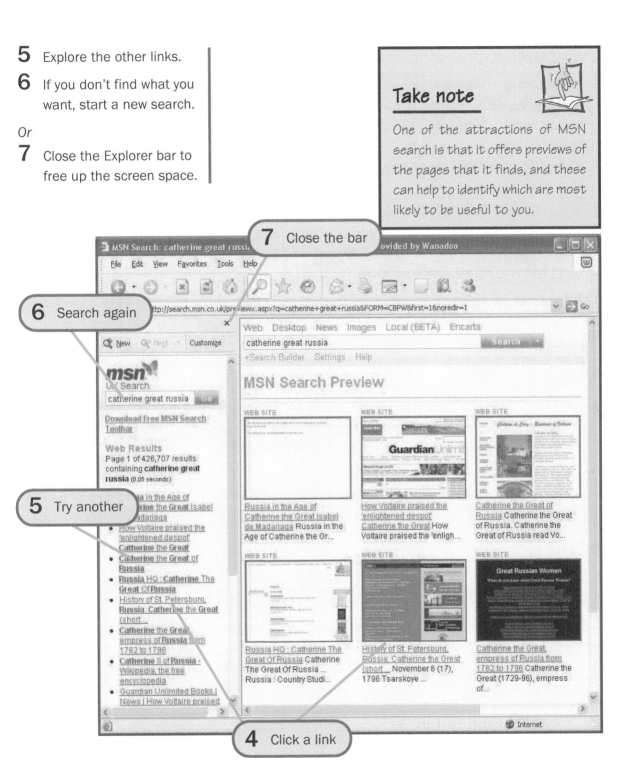

7 Close the bar

6 Search again

5 Try another

4 Click a link

Exercises

1 Start Internet Explorer and go online, if necessary.

2 Go to Google at www.google.com or www.google.co.uk. Think of two actors or singers who sometimes, but not always, work together. Run a simple search on the first, then do a search with in those results for the second name. Has this found pages about films or recordings that they have made together?

3 Run an advanced search at Google to find Word files written in the last 3 months about your country's football team, containing the words 'training' or 'coaching'. If you don't find any, try a longer time span.

4 Pick a topic from your own hobby or interests – something fairly unusual or specialised – and run a search for it at Google, AltaVista and Excite. Look at the first five results from each engine. How many of each were relevant and useful?

5 Repeat 4, but run the search from within Internet Explorer. Does this produce better or worse results? Does the Explorer bar make it easier to browse through the results?

5 Data from the Web

Saving pages

Page files are erased from the History list after a while. If you want to keep pages for long-term reference, save them on disk. They can be saved in four formats:

♦ **Web Page, complete** saves the page as an htm file, and saves any pictures, sounds and other content in a folder. This has the same name as the page with _files_ added.

♦ **Web Archive** also saves the text and other content, but packed into a single file.

♦ **Web Page, HTML only** save the text and HTML tags.

♦ **Text File** saves only the text.

1 From the **File** menu select **Save As ...**

2 Set the folder and filename.

3 Set the **Save as type**.

4 Click [Save] .

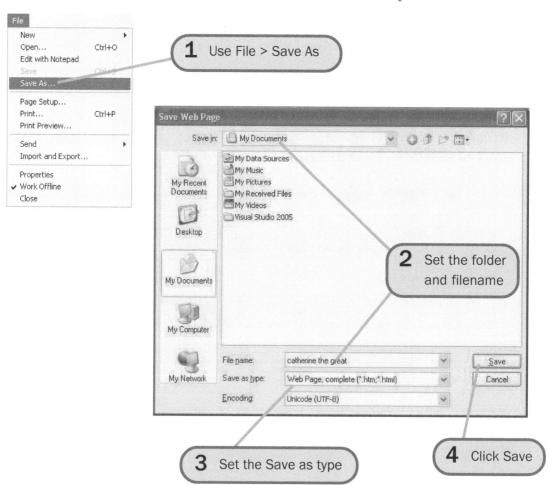

1 Use File > Save As

2 Set the folder and filename

3 Set the Save as type

4 Click Save

Opening saved pages

1 Open the **File** menu and select **Open**...

2 Type in the path and filename if you know it.

Or

3 Click Browse...

4 Locate the file and click Open.

5 Click OK.

If a page has been saved, you do not need to be on-line to view it again – though you will only get the full display if it was saved complete or as an archive.

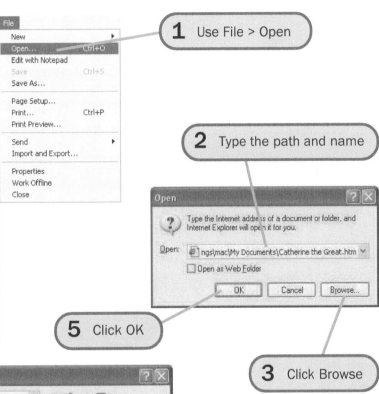

1 Use File > Open

2 Type the path and name

3 Click Browse

5 Click OK

Tip

Unless the path and filename are very short and simple, e.g. A:\mypage.htm, it is usually quicker to browse for the file.

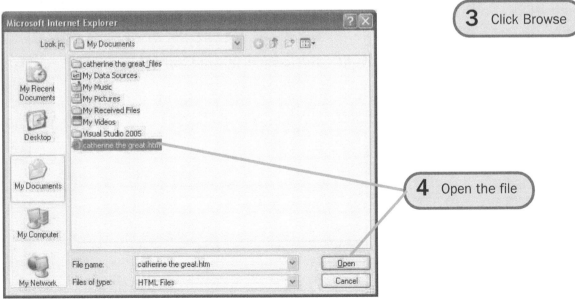

4 Open the file

Text from web pages

If you want to save all the text from a page, it is simplest to use the File > Save As command and select the Save As Text option. If you only want part of the text, it may be simpler to Copy and Paste it into a word-processor and save from there.

Basic steps

1 Select the text to be saved.

2 Open the **Edit** menu and select **Copy** or press [**Ctrl**] + [**C**].

3 Switch to your word-processor.

4 Click 🖹 or press [**Ctrl**] + [**V**].

5 Save the document as normal.

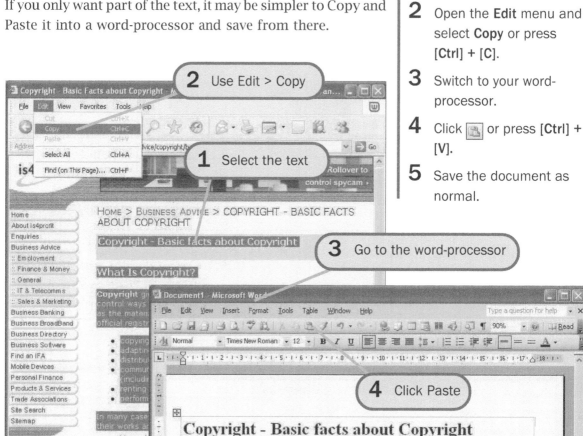

Take note

If the text has any decoration or embedded images, they will all be formatted into a table when pasted into Word.

58

Basic steps

1 Point to the image. A small toolbar will appear at the top left. Click 🖫.

Or

2 Right-click on the image and select **Save Picture As...** from the menu.

3 At the **Save As** dialog box, save the file as normal.

Individual images can be saved to disk very easily – if anything, too easily. Remember that, unless the site owners have waived their copyright, you cannot use these images in any commercial form. And yes, the owner of the page shown here has waived her copyright for its use in this book. See more of Iwona Botton's artwork at http://colorado.atspace.com.

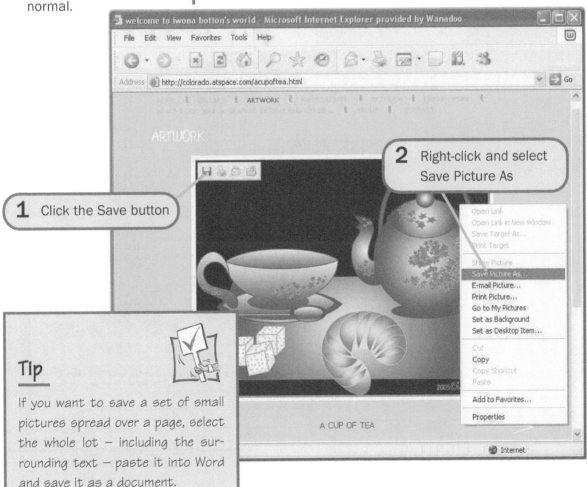

1 Click the Save button

2 Right-click and select Save Picture As

Tip

If you want to save a set of small pictures spread over a page, select the whole lot – including the surrounding text – paste it into Word and save it as a document.

Printing web pages

Web pages are normally designed to be seen on screen – not on paper. Before printing anything it is usually a good idea to use the Print Preview facility to see how it will come out, and how many pages it will take. It is surprising how often there is a last page with nothing relevant on it.

1 Open the **File** menu and select **Print Preview...**

2 Scroll through and decide which pages you want to print.

3 To print the whole page, click Print... .

Or

4 For a controlled print, click Close and use the the **File** > **Print** approach.

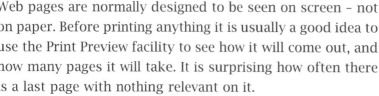

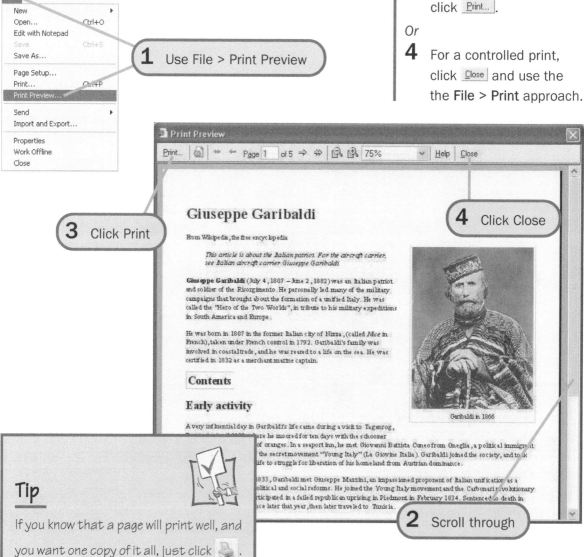

Tip

If you know that a page will print well, and you want one copy of it all, just click 🖶.

60

Basic steps

1 If you want to print a part of the page, select it first.

2 Open the **File** menu and select **Print ...**

3 At the **Print** dialog box, select the **Page Range**: **All**, **Selection**, or **Pages** giving the page number or range, e.g. 2-4.

4 If you have several printers, pick one.

5 Set the **Number of copies** to print more than one.

6 Click [Print].

Controlled printing

The Print dialog box gives you control over your printing.

If you do not want the whole of the web page, you can select part of it before you start to print, or use the Print Preview to work out which printed pages you will want.

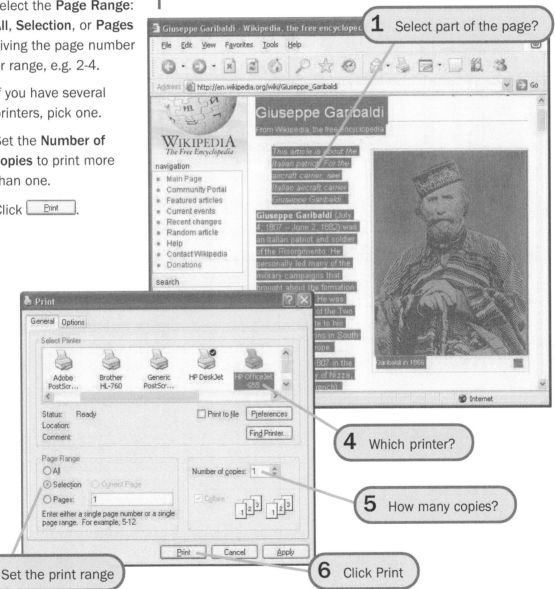

1 Select part of the page?

4 Which printer?

5 How many copies?

3 Set the print range

6 Click Print

AutoComplete

Internet Explorer likes to save you work! The AutoComplete feature offers to complete things for you as you start to type, suggesting words that you have typed previously and that began in the same way. It can complete:

◆ addresses, when you type them into the Address bar;

◆ data entered into forms, e.g. your name, address and similar details;

◆ user names and passwords.

You can decide which of these can be completed for you.

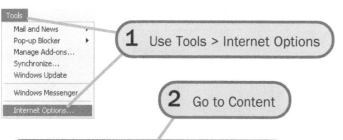

Basic steps

1 Open the **Tools** menu and select **Internet Options...**

2 Go to the **Content** tab.

3 Click AutoComplete....

4 Tick the boxes for the item that you want to be AutoCompleted.

5 Click OK to close the **AutoComplete Settings** dialog box.

6 Click OK.

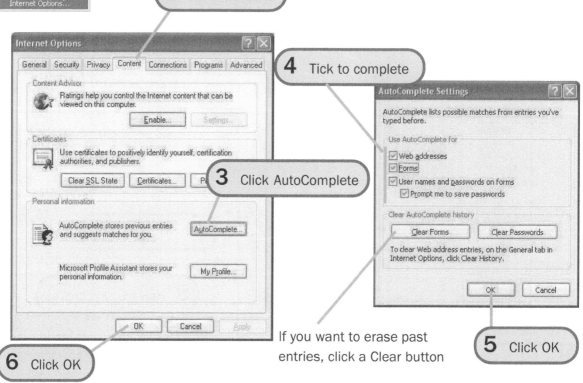

If you want to erase past entries, click a Clear button

Downloading files

Tip

If the lines to the site are busy, the download speed may be very slow. At times like this, it is often better cancel the download, to write down the URL, and try again later.

Beware viruses

As a general rule, if you only download files from well-established web sites, you shouldn't have any trouble as the organisers of these sites check files for viruses before putting them onto their systems! Be more wary of downloading from an individual's site, especially if they seem to be offering something very special for free! For safety, install anti-virus software on your system and check your downloads.

There's lots of software available for download from the Net. It falls into three categories:

♦ **Freeware** is there for the taking. People give software away from goodwill, or to promote themselves or their commercial products. Just because it is free does not mean it is no good – some excellent programs, including the Linux operating system are freeware!

♦ **Shareware** can be tried for free, but you must pay (usually around £20) for continued use. Shareware worth a look includes WinZip, the file compression utility, and PaintShop Pro, an excellent graphics package.

♦ **Demos**, also known as 'crippleware', give you a taste of what a program can do, but prevent you from doing some key tasks, such as saving or printing.

The software downloads in one of three forms:

♦ **Ready-to-run programs in a single file** – just click and go! If you intend to keep the program, move it out of the temporary folder into safer storage.

♦ **Zip-compressed files** – which can be unpacked by Windows XP. (If you have an earlier version of Windows, you will need WinZip to unpack them.) These usually have a set of installation files, and you must then run the **Setup** or **Install** file to get the actual program.

♦ **Self-extracting Zip files** – these have been created by WinZip, but have the unpacking routines built into them. When you run a self-extracting Zip file, the constituent files will normally be unpacked into the same folder. If these are the program files, you may want to set up a new folder for them and move them into it. If they are installation files, you will be prompted to choose a folder during installation. The installation files can then be deleted from your temporary folder.

Shareware at c|net

Basic steps

One of the best places for shareware (and freeware) programs is **download.com**. This is run by c|net which also provides a range of other services to Internet users.

To find software, either browse through the categories or run a search by typing its name or words that might appear in its brief description, into the Search field. In the example, a search for 'gif animation windows' found nearly 100 Windows packages for creating or manipulating animated GIF images, ranging from the free and cheerful to professional software.

1 Go to:
   www.download.com

2 In the **Search** slot, type the program name or a descriptive word.

3 Click **Go!**

4 Read the descriptions to find the right file.

5 Click on the **Download** button to start.

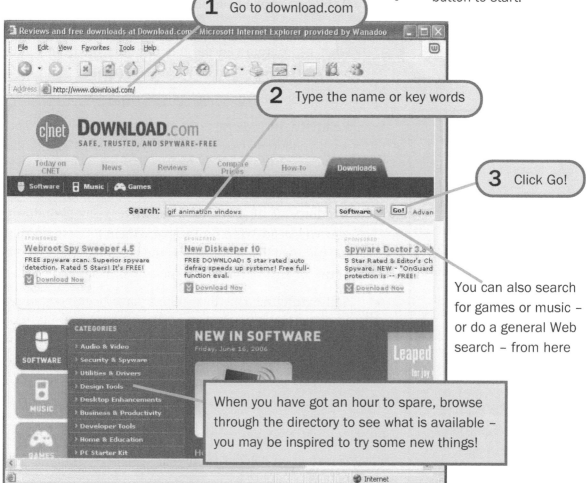

1 Go to download.com

2 Type the name or key words

3 Click Go!

You can also search for games or music – or do a general Web search – from here

When you have got an hour to spare, browse through the directory to see what is available – you may be inspired to try some new things!

64

6 Select the **Save** option and choose a folder in which to save it.

7 After the download is complete, locate the file and uncompress it or run it to install the software.

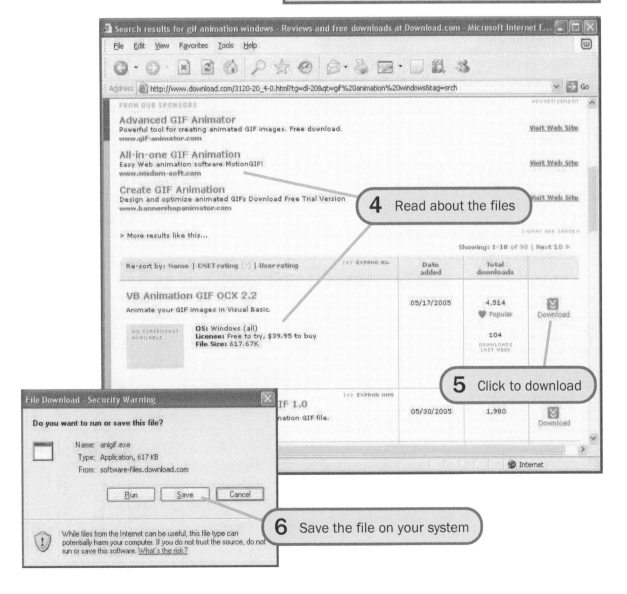

Search results for gif animation windows - Reviews and free downloads at Download.com - Microsoft Internet E...

File   Edit   View   Favorites   Tools   Help

Address http://www.download.com/3120-20_4-0.html?tg=dl-20&qt=gif%20animation%20windows&tag=srch   Go

FROM OUR SPONSORS   ADVERTISEMENT

Advanced GIF Animator
Powerful tool for creating animated GIF images. Free download.   Visit Web Site
www.gif-animator.com

All-in-one GIF Animation
Easy Web animation software MotionGIF!   Visit Web Site
www.wisdom-soft.com

Create GIF Animation
Design and optimize animated GIFs Download Free Trial Version   Visit Web Site
www.bannershopanimator.com   **4** Read about the files

> More results like this...

WHAT ARE THESE?

Showing: 1-10 of 98 | Next 10 >

Re-sort by: Name | CNET rating [?] | User rating   [+] EXPAND ALL   Date added   Total downloads

VB Animation GIF OCX 2.2   05/17/2005   4,514

Animate your GIF images in Visual Basic.   ♥ Popular   Download

NO SCREENSHOT AVAILABLE   **OS:** Windows (all)   104
                            License: Free to try, $39.95 to buy   DOWNLOADS LAST WEEK
                            File Size: 617.67K

5 Click to download

File Download - Security Warning

Do you want to run or save this file?   [+] EXPAND INFO

                                                         IF 1.0   05/30/2005   1,980
    Name: anigif.exe   nation GIF file.   Download
    Type: Application, 617 KB
    From: software-files.download.com

    [Run]   [Save]   [Cancel]
                                        6 Save the file on your system

⚠ While files from the Internet can be useful, this file type can potentially harm your computer. If you do not trust the source, do not run or save this software. What's the risk?

🌐 Internet

Antivirus software

If you are going to connect your PC to the Internet, you really ought to install antivirus software. If you are careful about what you download and what files you open, you may never need it, but it only takes one mistake and one bit of bad luck to get an infection. And it can take a lot of work to clean up your system and restore things afterwards.

The examples here use EZ Antivirus, but all good antivirus software offers the same facilities and works in much the same way. There are four key operations:

◆ scan the entire computer – a lengthy job, best done when the PC is not being used for anything else;

◆ scan files and e-mail messages as they are downloaded

◆ scan a selected file or folder;

◆ update the virus database – new viruses are produced all the time, and the software needs to be told how to recognise and deal with them.

Apart from scanning selected files/folders, all these jobs can be automated.

■ **Scan the system**

1 Run the program, from the Start menu or the icon on the Taskbar.

2 Click **Scan My Computer**. Do something else for a while so the software can scan undisturbed. If a virus is found, it will be dealt with and you will be informed.

■ **Schedule scans**

3 Click **Schedule a Scan**.

4 Turn on regular scanning and set the time for the first and the frequency, then click **OK**.

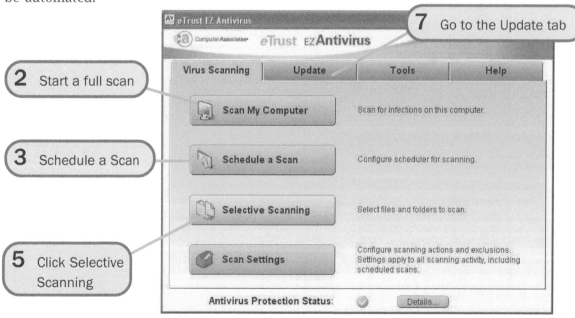

- **Scan a file**
5 Click **Selective Scanning**.
6 Select the file(s) to check and click **Scan**.

- **Schedule updates**
7 Go to the **Update** tab and click **Schedule update**.
8 Set it to update **auto-matically** or scheduled, giving its start time and frequency.
9 Click **OK**.

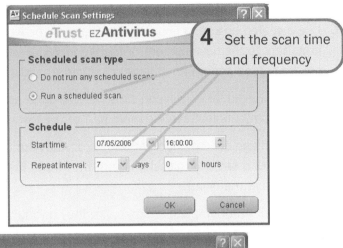

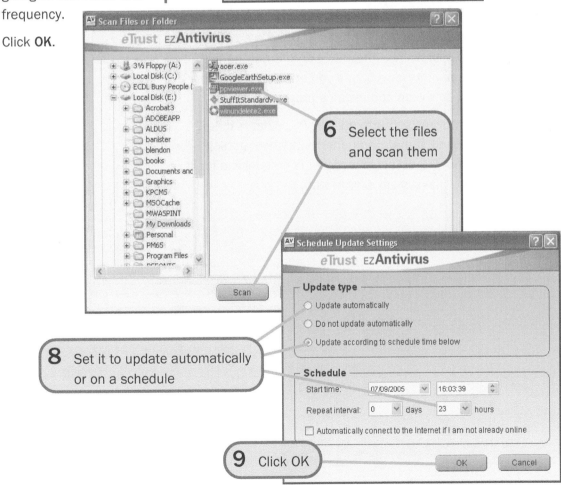

Exercises

1 Start Internet Explorer and go online, if necessary.

2 Use a search engine to find why Tim Berners-Lee was so important to the development of the World Wide Web. Locate a good page, with at least one picture, and save it.

3 Go to Wikipedia, at en.wikipedia.org and find the article on the dot-com bubble. Save the main part of the text.

4 Use the Image search option at Google or AltaVista to find a picture of a large tortoiseshell butterfly. (Aren't they lovely!) Save the picture.

5 Check your AutoComplete settings. Are they as you want them to be?

6 Go to download.com and see what sort of software – freeware and shareware – they have on offer. If there is something that interests you, and you are working on your own PC, then download and install a program.

7 Explore the antivirus software on your PC. What is there? How does it work? If there isn't any, think about getting some if it's your PC, or talk to whoever is responsible for it to find out how the system is protected.

6 E-mail software

Outlook (Express)

This book assumes that your e-mail software is either Outlook or Outlook Express – the two most widely used programs. As Outlook Express is the most common, most of the examples in the next three chapters are drawn from that software.

Outlook Express

Outlook Express is the mail and news application that comes with Internet Explorer. It is basically a simple piece of software, designed to do one job – to handle messages sent through the e-mail system – and it does it well.

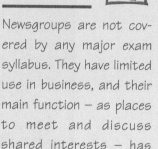

Take note

Newsgroups are not covered by any major exam syllabus. They have limited use in business, and their main function – as places to meet and discuss shared interests – has been largely taken over by blogs and chat rooms.

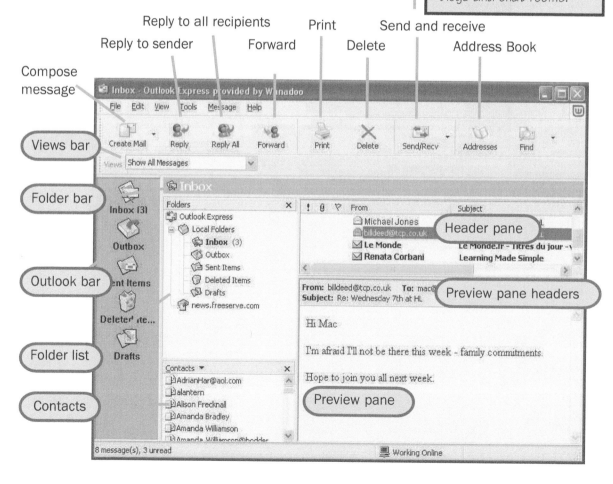

Reply to all recipients

Reply to sender

Print

Send and receive

Forward

Delete

Address Book

Compose message

Views bar

Folder bar

Outlook bar

Folder list

Contacts

Header pane

Preview pane headers

Preview pane

Outlook

Outlook is the e-mail program in the Microsoft Office suite. In fact, it can handle more than just e-mail – it is a personal organiser package that can also be used to plan your time and arrange meetings with others. However, we are only interested in its e-mail system, so the first thing to do is configure it to focus on that.

Drafts (messages you have saved, to finish and send later)

Inbox (incoming messages) – the number shows how many messages are unread

Outbox (messages waiting to be sent)

Sent Items (copies of messages you send)

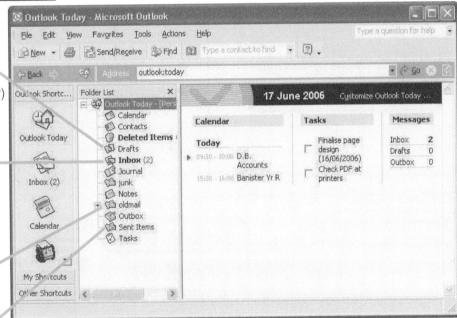

Outlook and e-mail

If you are only using Outlook for e-mail, it may help to turn off those screen elements that you aren't using. Open the View menu and clear the tick from the Outlook Bar, and from the Advanced toolbar on the Toolbars submenu.

Display options

The only fixed part of the window is the Header pane - all the rest are optional. As the Folder and Outlook bars do the same job, turn one off. If the Preview Pane is turned off, a new window will open to display a message when you click on it.

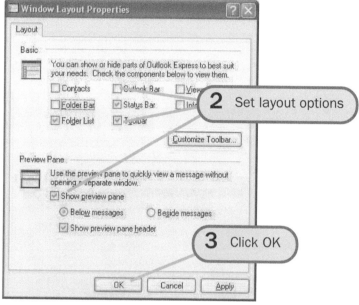

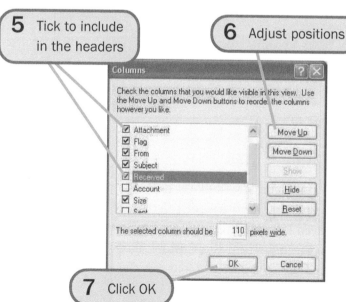

1 Open the **View** menu, select **Layout...**

2 Set the screen layout options.

3 Click OK.

4 Open the **View** menu, and select **Columns...**

5 Click on an item in the list to include it in the header display – clear the ticks from the items you do not want.

6 Adjust the positions with the **Move** buttons.

7 Click OK.

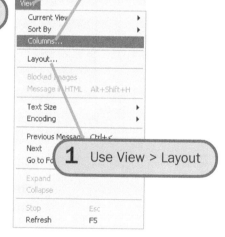

Basic steps

1 Open the **Tools** menu and select **Options...**

2 Click on a tab's label to bring it to the front.

3 Set your options – they are mainly on/off check-boxes. Note the ones covered in these pages.

4 Click [OK] when you have done.

Outlook Express has a lot of options that you can set to suit the way you handle e-mail.

Explore all the tabs – only the key ones have been covered here.

Most of us start at the Inbox

Do you use Messenger?

Pick up mail and alert you

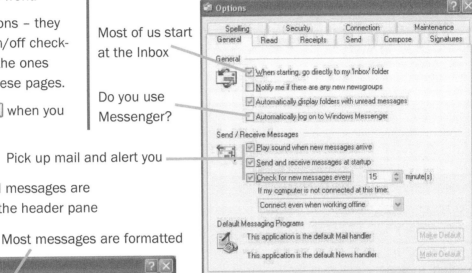

New and unread messages are listed in bold in the header pane

Most messages are formatted

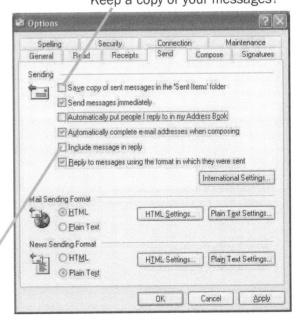

Keep a copy of your messages?

See page 80

You can add a 'signature' – your contact details or other text – to your messages

It's always worth spell-checking messages

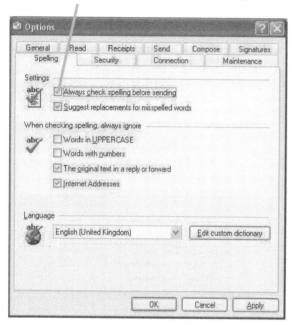

'Deleted' messages will sit in the Deleted folder until you delete them again – or you can have it emptied on exit

Type the signature here

Turn all these on to avoid nasty surprises in your Inbox

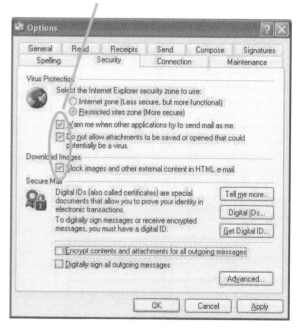

Basic steps

1 Open the **Help** menu and select **Contents and Index**.

2 Switch to the **Content** tab, if it is not on top.

3 Click 🕮 to open a 'book' of topics.

4 Click ❓ or 🔲 to display a Help page.

5 If the pages has a set of links to topics, click on one to reach its page.

The Help system in Outlook Express works in the same way as the one in Internet Explorer – only the content is different!

Browsing through the Contents is often the best way to get to know the system, but if you need specific Help, it is often quicker to try a key word in the Index or the Search tabs.

2 Go to Contents

Use the Options menu if you want to print a Help page

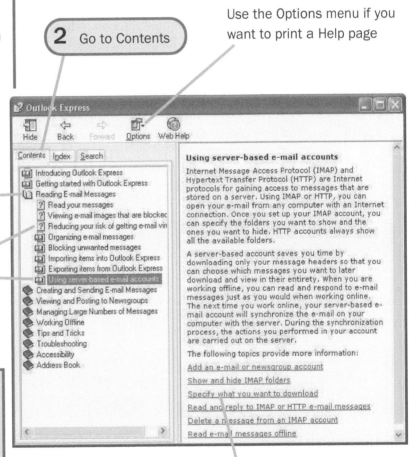

3 Open a book

4 Display a page

5 Click on a link

Tip

In the Contents list, look out for the Help pages with a 🔲 icon – this shows that the page contains a set of links to pages on the topic.

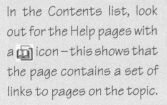

75

Exercises

1 Start Outlook Express (or Outlook) if necessary.

2 Identify the screen elements shown on pages 70 or 71. Do you have any toolbar buttons or features not shown there? If you do, use the Help system to find out about them.

3 Set the options to suit how you expect to use the software. Remember that they can be changed at any time, so do not worry about getting them right immediately.

4 Go to the Help system and find out how you can reduce the risk of getting viruses through e-mail messages.

5 If you have Outlook Express, use the Help system to find out about newsgroups. What newsgroups do you have access to through your Internet connection? How can you find this out, and how can you reach them?

7 Using e-mail

Mail accounts

To get e-mail, you need an e-mail account – obviously – and Outlook Express needs to know about it. There's a wizard to help you set up an account. This will run automatically the first time that you use Outlook, or can be run at any point to add a new account.

Before you start, get this information from your mail service provider and have it to hand:

◆ your user name and password;

◆ your e-mail name, e.g. JoSmith@mynet.co.uk;

◆ the names of your provider's incoming and outgoing mail servers – these may or may not be the same.

1 Open the **Tools** menu and select **Accounts...**

2 At the **Internet Accounts** dialog box, click [Add ▸] and select **Mail...**

3 Work through the wizard, giving your name, e-mail address and the server details at the prompts.

4 Click [Next >] after completing each stage.

5 Back at the dialog box, click [Close].

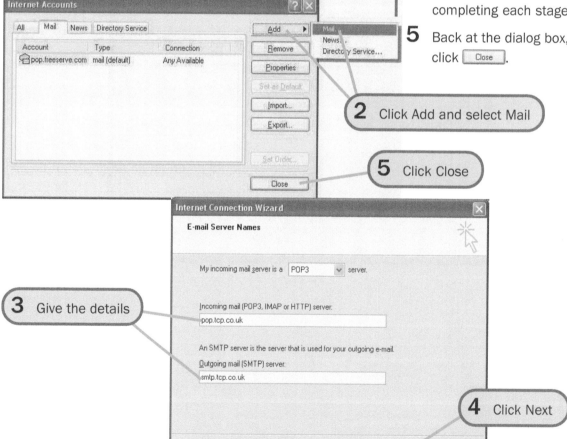

2 Click Add and select Mail

5 Click Close

3 Give the details

4 Click Next

Reading your e-mail

1 If the Preview pane is not open, use **View > Layout** to turn it on.

2 Check that the **Inbox** is selected in the **Folders**.

3 Click **Send/Receive** to pick up your mail.

4 Click on a header to display its message in the Preview pane.

Or

5 Double-click to open a new window to display the message.

Incoming messages are stored in the Inbox. The Header pane shows their basic details – who they are from, the subject and so on. When a header is selected here, its message is displayed in the Preview pane, if this is present.

Tip

If you get a lot of spam e-mail, turn off the Preview pane. This makes them easier to ignore! You just want to delete them, not read them.

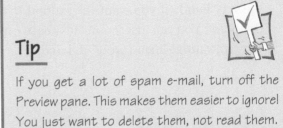

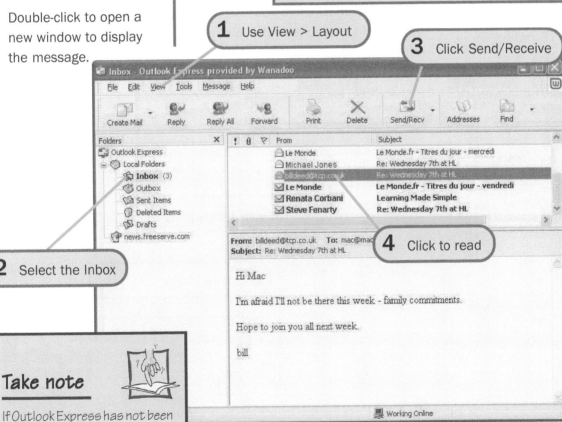

1 Use View > Layout

3 Click Send/Receive

2 Select the Inbox

4 Click to read

Take note

If Outlook Express has not been used before there should be a welcome message in the Inbox.

Replying

When you reply to an incoming message, the system will open the New Message window and copy the sender's address into the To: text box.

◆ The original message is normally also copied into the main text area with > at the start of each line. This can be very handy if you want to respond to the mail point-by-point. You can insert your text between the lines, and any unwanted lines can be deleted.

1 Select the message in the header pane.

2 Click 🔧 the Reply button.

3 Delete any unwanted headers or other text and add your own comments.

4 Add your own text.

5 Click 📧 .

5 Click Send

If you want the sender's address, right-click on it and select **Add to Address Book** – though if the option to add when replying is turned on, you don't need to do this

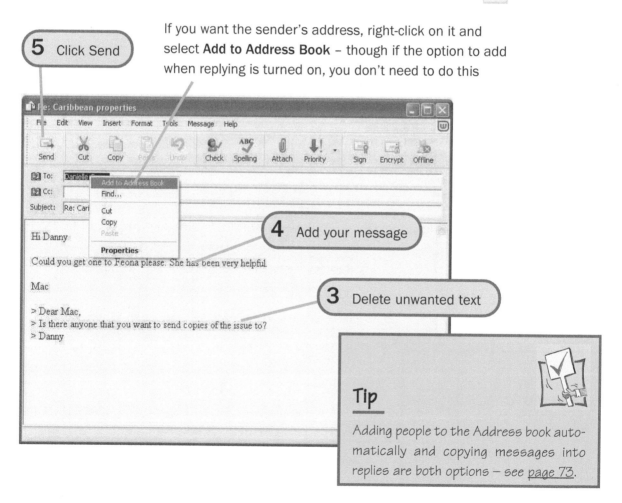

4 Add your message

3 Delete unwanted text

Tip

Adding people to the Address book automatically and copying messages into replies are both options – see page 73.

Forward

1 Select the message in the header pane.

2 Click ✉ the Forward button.

3 Type or select the address(es) of the recipient(s).

4 Delete any unwanted headers or other text and add your own comments.

5 Click 📧 .

You can send a message on to another person – perhaps after adding your own comments to it.

Reply to all

If you get a message that has been sent to several people, you can reply to all those listed in the **To:** and **Cc:** boxes. Click 📧 , instead of ✉ , and continue as for a normal reply. Your message will be copied to all the recipients of the original message.

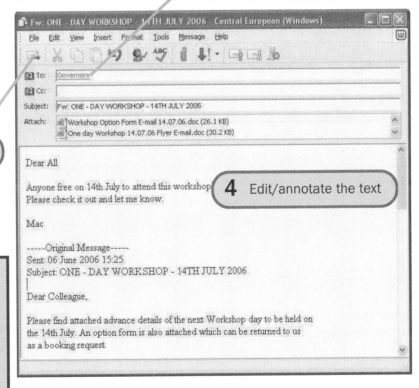

3 Type or select the recipients

5 Click Send

4 Edit/annotate the text

Take note

The Bcc: box is for 'Blind carbon copies'. Any Bcc: recipients are not listed on the copies sent to other people.

Sending messages

To send e-mail, all you need is the address – and something to say! Messages can be composed and sent immediately if you are online, or composed offline and stored for sending later.

To add impact, write your message on appropriate stationery! This has text formats and a background all ready for you.

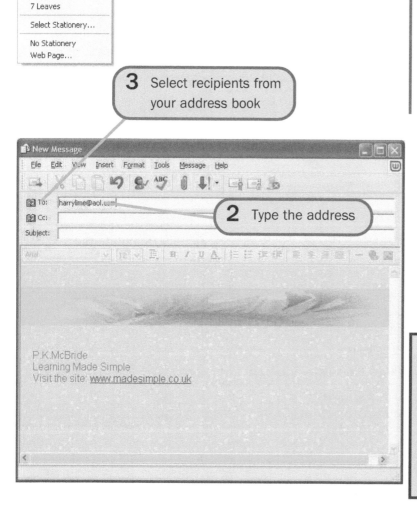

1 Select your stationery

3 Select recipients from your address book

2 Type the address

1 Click the arrow beside **Write Message** and select your stationery.

- Use **No stationery** – or click for plain paper.

2 Type the address in the **To:** slot.

Or

3 Click 📖 To: by the top line to open the **Select Recipients** dialog box.

4 Select a name and click the To: -> button, then OK to copy the address.

Take note

Subject lines are important as they help your recipients to organise their messages. Make them brief, but clear.

- To send copies, repeat from step 2 for the **Cc:** text box.

5 Type a **Subject**.

6 Type your message.

7 Click ⬛.

Or

8 Open the **File** menu and select **Send Message**, for immediate delivery, or **Send Later**.

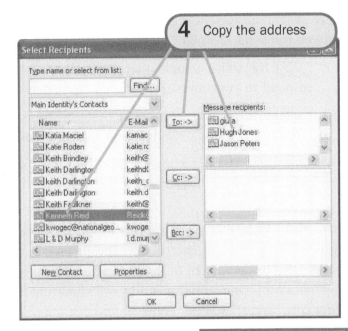

4 Copy the address

7 Send it

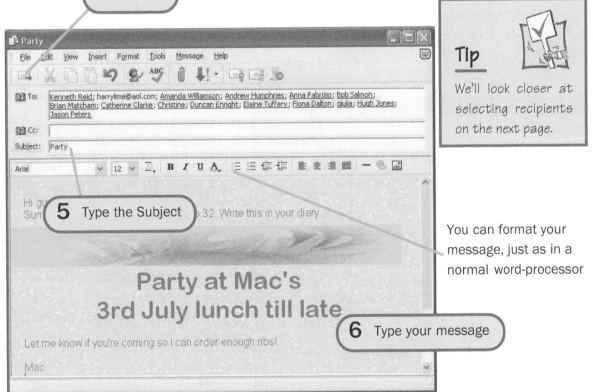

5 Type the Subject

6 Type your message

Tip

We'll look closer at selecting recipients on the next page.

You can format your message, just as in a normal word-processor

Selecting recipients

There are three types of recipients, i.e. there are three ways that you can send messages to people:

◆ `To: ->` for those people that you want to read and respond to your message.

◆ `Cc: ->` (Carbon copy) for those that you want to keep informed, but don't really expect them to reply.

◆ `Bcc: ->` (Blind carbon copy) sends copies to people without including their addresses in the messages that other people receive.

When this message is sent, Andrea, Chris, Dave, Anna and Cathy will all get a copy. Everyone will be able to see from the headers that it was written to Andrea and that Chris and Dave have had a copy. Only Anna and Cathy will know that they have had a copy, and they won't know about each other's.

Start to type the name here to scroll quickly down to the right part of the list

Starts the Find People routine – see page 91

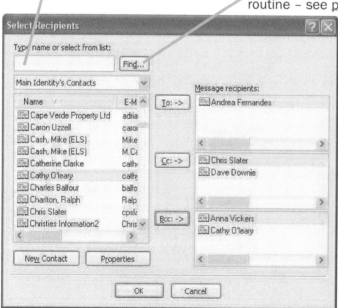

Take note

Blind carbon copies are mainly used for mailing lists (see page 92) where people do not want usually their addresses given strangers. When you are writing to an individual – as in the example here – you would not normally use Bcc. People should know who else is reading their mail.

Tip

If you put someone in the wrong category, you cannot move them. Select the name, press [Delete] and try again.

Basic steps

1 Start the spell checker – if necessary – by clicking the Spelling button.

2 When the spell checker finds a word it does not recognise, the Spelling dialog box will open.

3 To use a suggestion, pick one and click `Change`.

4 If the word is spelled correctly, click `Ignore`.

5 To add the word to the dictionary – so that it is recognised next time – click `Add`.

6 When the check is complete, click `OK`.

The spell checker

Most people treat e-mail is an informal, chatty means of communication – 'Hi' is a more common greeting that 'Dear sir'. But there's a difference between informal and sloppy. If a message has spelling mistakes, it is more likely to be mis-understood. And spelling mistakes are completely avoidable because there's a built-in spell checker.

You can set the spell checker to run automatically before a message is sent (see page 74), or run it yourself at any time.

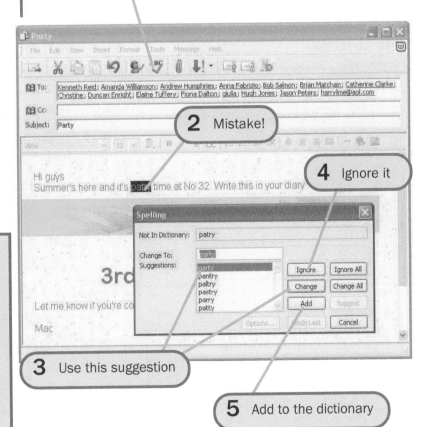

1 Start the checker

2 Mistake!

4 Ignore it

3 Use this suggestion

5 Add to the dictionary

Tip

The checker may well not recognise names, slang and technical jargon. Add words to the dictionary if you are likely to use them again in future.

Files by mail

Files of any type – graphics, word-processor and spreadsheet documents, audio and video clips – and URL links, can be attached to messages and sent by e-mail. Compared to sending files printed or on disk in the post, e-mail is almost always quicker, often more reliable and cheaper.

◆ If you use the Rich Text format, rather than plain text, you can also insert pictures directly into a message.

Basic steps

1 Compose the message.

2 From the **Insert** menu select **File Attachment...**

■ **To attach a file**

3 Browse for the file and click **Attach**.

■ **To insert a picture**

4 Open the **Format** menu and select **Rich Text**.

5 Browse for the picture source and click [OK].

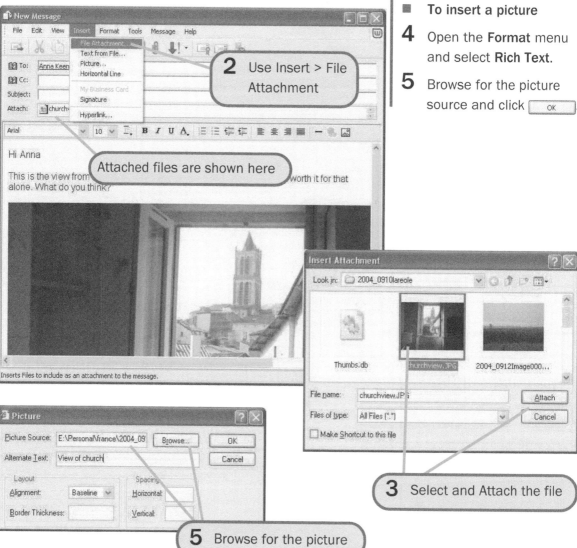

2 Use Insert > File Attachment

Attached files are shown here

3 Select and Attach the file

5 Browse for the picture

Basic steps

1 Click on the icon to open the menu.

2 Click on the name and the file will be opened in its linked application.

3 The system may check that you want to open the file – click [Open] if you are sure that it is safe.

Or

4 Select **Save Attachments** and save the file to disk.

Detaching files

Detaching files from messages used to be hard work – they had to be cut out from the text of the message and processed through special decoding software. With Outlook Express, it's a piece of cake. If the preview pane header bar is present, an attached file is shown by a paperclip icon. If it is not, you must open the message in its own window – the file will be listed in the Attach: line.

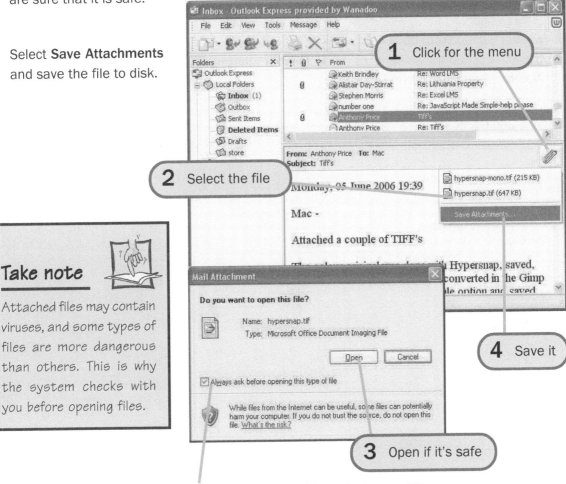

This can be cleared for safe types of files
– and image files cannot carry viruses

Take note

Attached files may contain viruses, and some types of files are more dangerous than others. This is why the system checks with you before opening files.

87

Exercises

1 Start Outlook Express, if necessary. Alert a friend that you are going to need their help – you have to have someone to write to and get messages from!

2 Send an e-mail to your collaborator, asking them to write to you. Use stationery and formatting if you like. Make sure that you type something meaningful in the Subject line, and check the spelling before you send it.

3 When you get a message from your friend, reply to it. If the original message is copied in, delete any of it that you do not want, then type your reply.

4 Send a file – a Word document or an image – to your friend. Describe the contents of the file in your message. Ask for an attached file in return.

5 When you get a message with an attachment, first save it in a suitable folder, then open it directly from the e-mail.

8 Organising e-mail

Address Book

Typing e-mail addresses is a pain – one slip and the mail comes bouncing back the next day with a 'recipient unknown' label. The simple solution is to use the Address Book. Type the address in once correctly – or add it when replying to a message (page 80) – and it's there whenever you want it.

(page 80)

Basic steps

Basic steps

1 Click the **Address Book** button .

2 Click [New] and select **New Contact...**

3 Enter the **First**, **Middle** and **Last** names – contacts are normally listed alphabetically by **Display name** (First + Last).

4 Type the address and click [Add].

5 If the person has several addresses, add them and set one as the **Default**.

6 Click [OK].

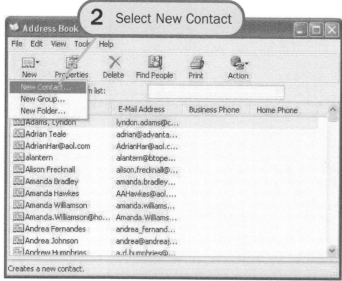

Other contact details can be added on these tabs

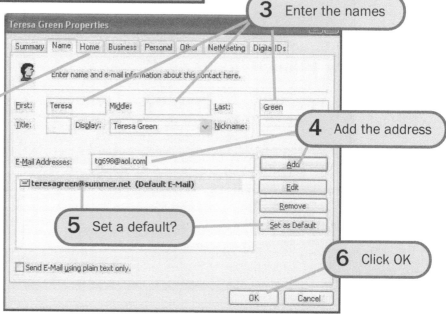

90

Finding an address

1 Start to type the name in the box above the list. The list will scroll down to those where the display name starts with the typed letters.

Or

2 Click 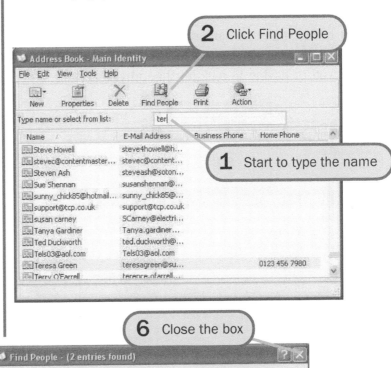 Find People .

3 At the **Find People** dialog box, type any part of the name, e-mail or other known details.

4 Click [Find Now].

5 Any matching entries will be listed in the lower pane. Double-click on the one you want, or select it and click [Properties].

6 Click ⊠ to close the dialog box.

No matter how many people you have in your Address Book, it's never hard to find one. You can run a simple search from the main page, or if that fails, use the Find People routine.

2 Click Find People

1 Start to type the name

6 Close the box

3 Enter known details

4 Click Find Now

5 Double-click to open

Groups

One of the big advantages that e-mail has over the telephone, fax or snail mail is that you can send messages to 1000 people as easily as you can send it to one. This is also one of the big disadvantages… (see page 97).

A group brings together any number of e-mail addresses under a single name, which you can select from your Address Book, instead of having to pick all the individual names.

■ **To create a group**

1 Open the Address Book.

2 Click [New] and select **New Group**.

3 Click [Select Members].

4 Work through the list of contacts, selecting each person in turn and clicking [Select ->].

5 Click [OK].

6 Back at the **Properties** dialog box, check the names. If one is there by mistake, select it and click [Remove].

2 Select New Group

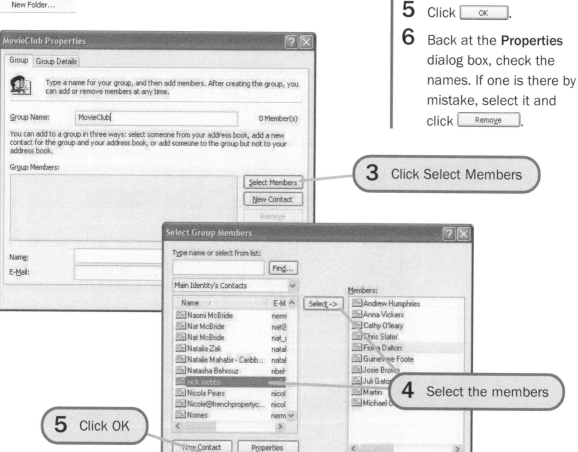

3 Click Select Members

4 Select the members

5 Click OK

92

7 Click [OK].

■ **To write to a group**

8 Start a new message. Type the group's name or click  and select it from the Address Book. If you do not want the group members to see each others' addresses, use send them as Bcc (see page 84).

9 Finish and send the message as usual.

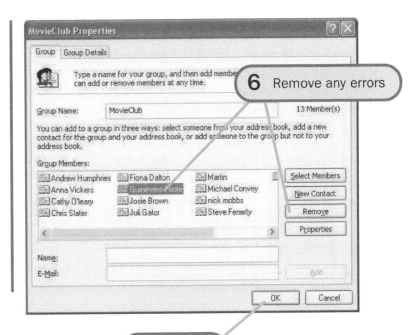

6 Remove any errors

7 Click OK

8 Use the group name

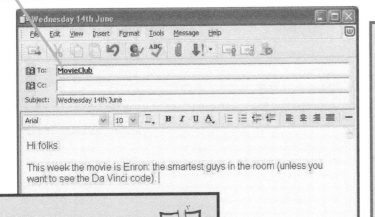

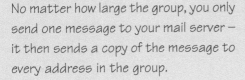

Take note

No matter how large the group, you only send one message to your mail server – it then sends a copy of the message to every address in the group.

Tip

You can add people to the group by typing their name and email address directly in, but that won't put them into your Address Book as individuals. If there is someone who is not yet in your book, use **New Contact** to create an Address Book entry for them.

Folders for mail

E-mail needs organising. Even with light use – say 2 or 3 incoming messages a day – there will be getting on for 1000 in the Inbox by the end of the year! Treat e-mail as you would snail mail. After you have read and replied to a message, throw it away or store it somewhere else if you want to keep it.

You can create folders at any time. As with folders in Windows Explorer, they can be created inside other folders if you want to subdivide areas.

Basic steps

1 Open the **File** menu, point to **New** and select **Folder...**

2 Type a suitable, meaningful name.

3 At the **Create Folder** dialog box, select the folder in which to create the new one – select **Local Folders** for a top-level one.

4 Click OK.

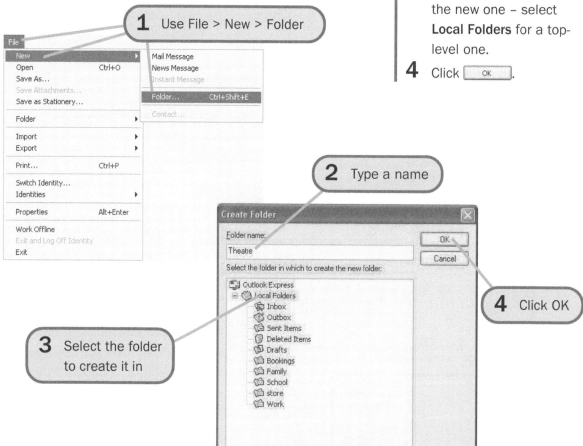

1 Use File > New > Folder

2 Type a name

3 Select the folder to create it in

4 Click OK

Moving messages

1 Select the message.

2 Drag it across to the folder and drop it in.

Or

3 Right-click on the mesage and select **Move to Folder...**

4 Select the folder and click [OK].

Once they are in place, it is simple to move messages out of the Inbox and into appropriate folders.

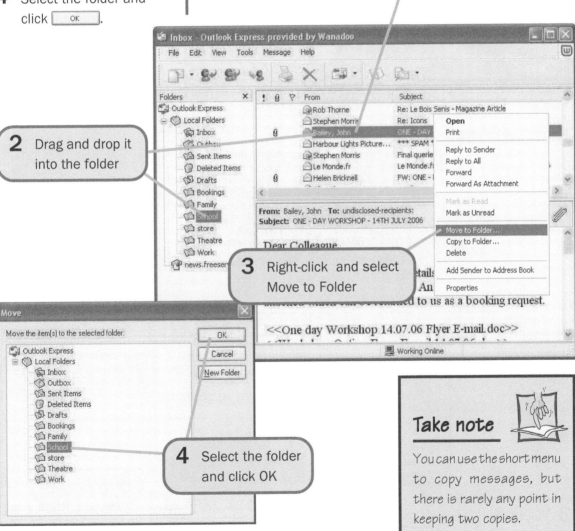

1 Select the message

2 Drag and drop it into the folder

3 Right-click and select Move to Folder

4 Select the folder and click OK

Take note

You can use the short menu to copy messages, but there is rarely any point in keeping two copies.

Printing messages

E-mail messages can be printed out if you need a permanent copy. The process is almost the same as printing web pages, except that Outlook Express does not offer a Print Preview facility.

Basic steps

1 Select the message.

2 Open the **File** menu and select **Print...**

3 At the **Print** dialog box, set the **Page Range**: **All**, **Selection**, or **Pages**.

4 Pick the printer.

5 Set the **Number of copies** if required.

6 Click ⬚ Print ⬚.

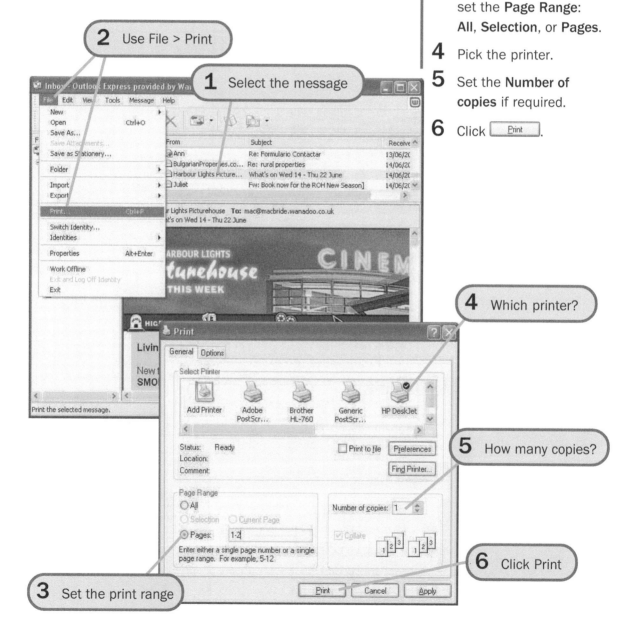

Message rules

1 On the **Tools** menu, point to **Message Rules** and select **Mail...** .

2 If you already have some rules, the **Message Rules** dialog box will open. Click New... .

3 At the **New Mail Rule** dialog box, select the **Condition** for the rule – how are messages selected?

4 If the condition needs to be defined, click on the underlined text.

5 At the definition dialog box, enter the values that you want the system to check for – type them and click Add .

6 Select the **Action** – what is to be done with them?

7 Click OK .

8 Back at the Message Rules dialog box, type a name for the rule.

9 Click OK .

In amongst the useful, interesting and necessary e-mail that you receive will be some spam (junk mail) – advertisements for real and imaginary goods, invitations to dubious web sites, and other attempts to part you from your money. The simplest way to deal with these is to select the messages by their subject/senders and delete them immediately.

If junk mail is a significant problem – particularly if a lot is coming from the same source – you might like to set up a message rule to deal with it. A rule is an instruction to Outlook Express to look out for a certain type of message, and to deal with it automatically. Typically, the rule will pick up messages from a named sender and delete them immediately.

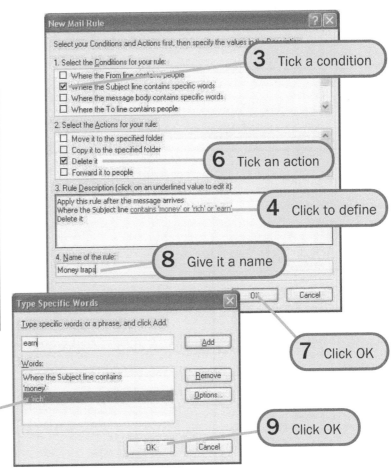

3 Tick a condition

6 Tick an action

4 Click to define

8 Give it a name

7 Click OK

5 Define the values to look for

9 Click OK

Rules from messages

You can create a message rule from a message. This works best when the rule is based on the sender, and you want to move their new messages directly into a specific folder, rather than sitting in the Inbox.

1 Select the message.

2 Open the **Message** menu and select **Create Rule From Message…**

3 Select the **Action**.

4 If the action needs to be defined, click on the underlined text.

5 Give it a name.

6 Click [OK].

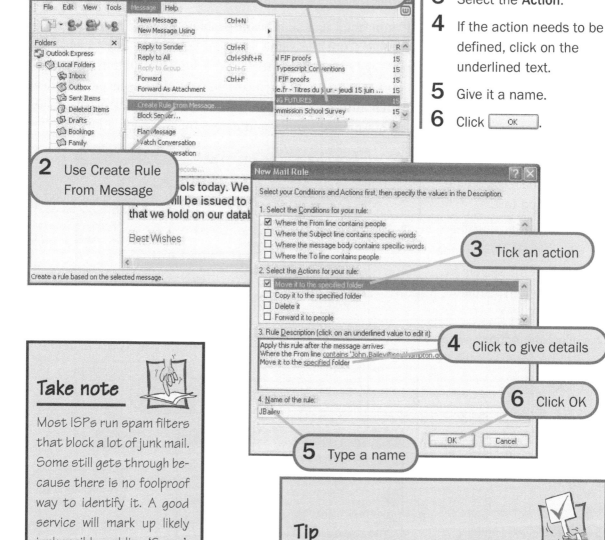

1 Select a message

2 Use Create Rule From Message

3 Tick an action

4 Click to give details

5 Type a name

6 Click OK

Take note

Most ISPs run spam filters that block a lot of junk mail. Some still gets through because there is no foolproof way to identify it. A good service will mark up likely junk mail by adding 'Spam', or something similar, to the Subject line.

Tip

If you do not want any more messages from someone, select a message and use Message> Block Sender…

E-tiquette rules

- **Small is beautiful.** Short messages are quick and cheap to download.

- **Test first.** When sending anything other than plain text, try a short test file first to make sure that the other person can receive it properly.

- **Zip it up!** If you are sending files, compress them with WinZip.

- **Subject matters!** Always type a Subject line so that the other person can identify the message.

- **Short signatures.** If you create a signature, keep it short.

- **Don't SHOUT.** Using capitals is known as shouting. It's OK to emphasise the odd word this way, but don't shout whole messages.

When you send someone a paper letter, you know that what they receive will be the same as you send, and if you enclose lots of material, you will pay the extra postage.

E-mail is different. Your recipients actively download your messages, which takes time and can cost money (see below). Further, if they are using different mail software to yours, it can affect the appearance – and sometimes the delivery – of your messages.

Formatted text

Most modern e-mail software can display formatted text, but few people bother with formatting. The essence of e-mail is that it is quick and informal – plain text is the norm. Save your fancy stationery for special announcements and greetings.

Size

Some e-mail systems set a limit to the size of messages, typically 10Mb. You won't be writing messages this big, but if you attach several large photos or a video this could push it over the limit.

File size is still a factor if your recipient has a dial-up connection. Large files take time to download, and this may add to their phone bills. On a standard phone line, e-mail usually comes in at around 3Kb per second, or 1Mb in 5 minutes. If they are on broadband, the cost is not affected by usage and time is hardly an issue as 1Mb will download in a few seconds.

You can reduce the size by compressing files, either with Window's Send to Compressed folder facility, or WinZip software. Graphics and documents files can often be reduced to 10% or less of their original size this way. Even executable files – the most difficult to compress – show some reduction.

Subject lines

A clear Subject line identifies a message. Your recipients need this when the mail arrives, to see which to deal with first – and which to ignore completely! They also need it when organising old mail, so that they know which to delete and which to place in what folder.

Emphasis

If your recipient's mail system can handle formatted text, then you can use <u>underline</u> or **bold** for emphasis. If you are sending plain text, and want to make a word stand out, enclose it in *asterisks* or _underscores_, or write it in CAPITALS.

Smileys

E-mail messages tend to be brief, and as your receipients cannot see your expression or hear the tone of your voice, there is a possibility of being misunderstood – especially when joking. Smileys, also known as *emoticons,* are little pictures, composed of ASCII characters, that can help to convey your meaning.

The basic smiley of :-) is the one you will see most often, though there are many other weird and wonderful smileys around. Here are a few of the more common ones.

:-)	It's a joke
'-)	Wink
:-(	I'm feeling sad
:-o	Wow!
:-C	I don't believe it!
(-:	I'm left handed
%-)	I've been staring at a screen for hours!
8-)	I'm wearing sunglasses

Take note

If you want to add your signature to messages, go to the Signatures tab in the Options dialog box (see page 74) and type one there. If you prefer, you can create the file in a word-processor, saving it as plain text, then link that file at the Signatures tab.

Abbreviations

BTW	By The Way
BWQ	Buzz Word Quotient
FYI	For Your Information
IMHO	In My Humble Opinion (ironic)
POV	Point Of View
TIA	Thanks In Advance
TTFN	Ta Ta For Now
WRT	With Reference To
<g>	Grin

If you are an indifferent typist, or like to keep your messages short, or are likely to be getting mail from old 'netties', then it's worth learning a few of the standard abbreviations. You will also find these used in real-time conferences and chat lines, and in newsgroup articles.

If you want to track down more abbreviations or the acronyms used elsewhere in the computing world, an excellent list called Babel is maintained by Irving and Richard Kind. Get a copy at this URL:

http://www.geocities.com/ikind_babel/babel/babel.html

Signatures

A signature can be added to the end of every message. In Outlook Express, this can be created in the Options dialog box (see page 74) or it can be created in a word-processor and saved as a plain text file. It will normally contain your name, and any other contact details you want to give. People's signatures often also contain a favourite quote, advert, or a picture or name created from ASCII characters. e.g.

Example 1

```
- - - - - - - - - - - - -
P.K. McBride    |macbride@tcp.co.uk
Computing's Made Simple at http://www.madesimple.co.uk
- - - - - - - - - - - - -
```

Example 2

```
              _\ | /_
             @ @    =
_____ooO_(_)_Ooo_____
Roger Wallace
```

Exercises

1 Start Oultook (Express) and open the Address Book.

2 Look through the entries. Are there any of your contacts missing? Do you have their addresses? If so, use the New Contact routine to add them now.

3 Are there any entries in the book that shouldn't be there? Old addresses that are no longer used, or addresses of people to whom you once replied but will not write to again? Select and delete any surplus entries.

4 Create a new group called 'friends' and add to it those of your friends that you would invite to parties or send christmas greetings to. Next time you need to contact them, you can do it by picking a single entry out of the book. (But don't just mail for the sake of it – that's spam.)

5 Select two different messages, preferably one short and one long, and print them.

6 Create a message rule to delete messages offering stocks and shares tips – they are all spam. Set it to look for key words in the Subject.

7 Read the etiquette and try to follow it in your mailings.

9 Creating web pages

HTML

Most access providers offer their customers the facilities to set up their own home pages. People use them to advertise their work, their products, their clubs, their hobbies – or just themselves!

HTML – HyperText Markup Language – is the system used to produce Web pages. Essentially, it is a set of tags (codes) that specify text styles, draw lines, display images, handle URL links and the other features that create Web pages. It is not difficult to use. There are only a limited number of tags and they follow fairly strict rules. All tags are enclosed in <angle brackets> to mark them off from the text, and they are normally used in pairs – one at the start and one at the end of the text that they affect. For example:

```
<H1> This is a main heading </H1>
```

Notice that the closing tag is the same as the opener, except that it has a forward slash at the start.

All pages have the same outline structure:

```
<HTML>
<HEAD>
   <TITLE>My Gnome Page</TITLE>
</HEAD>
<BODY>
   This page is under construction
</BODY>
</HTML>
```

The whole text is enclosed by <HTML> and </HTML> tags.

The <HEAD> area holds information about the page, and is not displayed – though the Title does appear in the browser's Title bar when loaded. This can be left blank.

The <BODY> area is where the main code goes.

The HTML file that produces the web page is plain text, and can be written in Notepad (which is small and efficient) or WordPad or Word, but must be saved as plain text.

Basic steps

1 Type your HTML text into NotePad or other word-processor.

2 Save the document with an '.HTM' extension, e.g. 'MYPAGE.HTM'. If you are not using NotePad, set the **Save as type** to .txt.

3 Start your browser – don't go online – and use **Open > File** to load in the document.

4 Check the display and return to NotePad to enhance and improve! Save it, then refresh the browser display to see the new version.

Take note

HTML is easy to learn and 'hand-coding' – creating a page from scratch – can give you better control over the appearance of your pages, but it is simpler and quicker to create Web pages with a dedicated HTML editor, or even with Word.

104

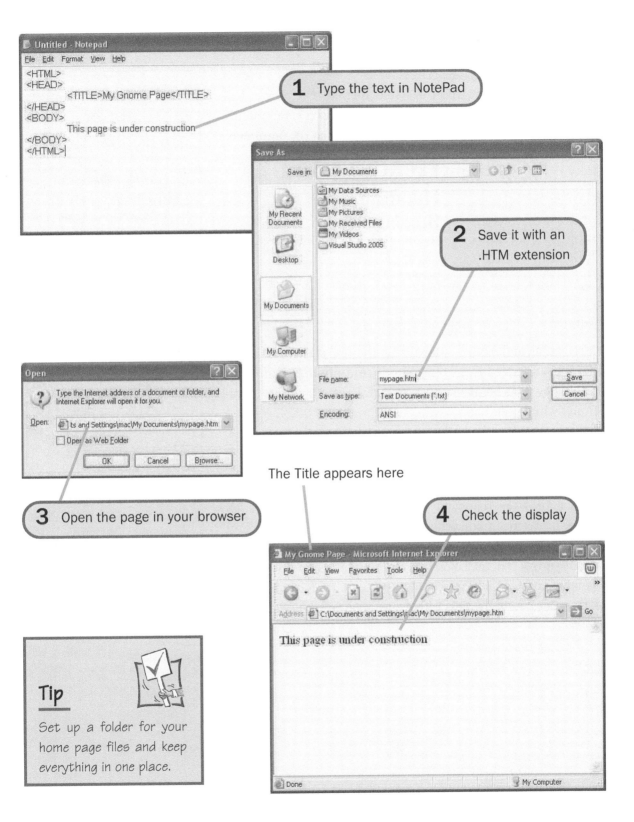

1 Type the text in NotePad

```
<HTML>
<HEAD>
        <TITLE>My Gnome Page</TITLE>
</HEAD>
<BODY>
        This page is under construction
</BODY>
</HTML>
```

2 Save it with an .HTM extension

3 Open the page in your browser

The Title appears here

4 Check the display

This page is under construction

Tip

Set up a folder for your home page files and keep everything in one place.

Text tags

The simplest tags are the ones that format text. These will produce six levels of headings, a small, italicised style (mainly used for e-mail addresses), and bold and italic for emphasis.

<H1>	</H1>	# Heading 1
<H2>	</H2>	## Heading 2
<H3>	</H3>	### Heading 3
<H4>	</H4>	**Heading 4**
<H5>	</H5>	**Heading 5**
<H6>	</H6>	**Heading 6**
<B>	</B>	**Bold**
<I>	</I>	*Italic*
<Address>	</Address>	*Small italic style*

The Heading and Address tags break the text up into separate lines, but untagged text appears as a continuous stream – no matter how you lay it out in NotePad. Create separate paragraphs with these tags:

<P>	Start a new paragaph with a space before and after
</P>	End of paragraph (optional)
 	Start a new line without a space before it

When a browser reads an HTML document, it ignores all spaces (apart from a single space between words), tabs and new lines. What this means is that it doesn't matter how you lay out your HTML text. You can indent it, and add line breaks to make it easier for you to read, but it won't affect what your readers see – only the tags affect the layout of the page in the browser.

```
<HTML>
<HEAD>
  <TITLE>My Gnome Page</TITLE>
</HEAD>
<BODY>
  <H1>My Gnome Page</H1>
  <H3>Hello and welcome</H3>
  <H2>Gnomic sayings</H2>
  <P>Every gnome should have one.
  <P>There's gno place like Gnome. (Old Alaskan proverb)
  <P>Gnome is where the heart is.
  <H2>Gnome computing</H2>
  Lots of links to go here!
  <BR>
  <H4>This page is under construction</H4>
  <ADDRESS>Ingrid Bottomlow </ADDRESS>
  <ADDRESS>Last Update: Mudday of this week</ADDRESS>
</BODY>
</HTML>
```

Compare the HTML code with the screen display and note the effect of the <H..> <ADDRESS> <P> and
tags.

Why do these lines have tags at both ends? What would happen if both were enclosed in one set of <ADDRESS> </ADDRESS> tags?

Take note

You don't have to use images to produce good-looking pages. Pages that consist only of text are faster to download – and you can make them attractive using just colour and headings.

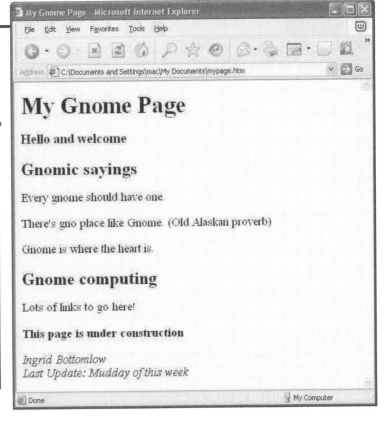

Colours

Text-only pages are fast to load, but can be a bit boring. Colour adds impact to your screens, without adding to the loading time.

Colours are defined by the values of their Red, Green and Blue components – given in that order and in hexadecimal digits. These values can be anything from 00 to FF, but are best set at 00 (off), 80 (half/dark) or FF (full power/bright), e.g.:

FFFF00

gives Red and Green at full, with no Blue, resulting in Yellow. Combinations of 00, 80 and FF values should come out true on all screens – other values may not.

Modern browsers recognise a set of common colour names, which you can use in your code. But if you want to create specific shades, you will have to work out their hex values.

BODY colours

The colours of the background and text of the page can be set by the BGCOLOR and TEXT options in the BODY tag.

```
<BODY BGCOLOR = "#FFFFFF" TEXT = "#008000">
```
This sets the background to White and the text to Dark Green.

Values are normally enclosed in "quotes" with a # at the start to show that they are hexadecimal. These can be omitted, TEXT = 008000 works just as well.

FONT COLOR

At any point on the page, you can change the colour of the text with the tag:

```
<FONT COLOR = "#Value" >
```
The colour is used for all following text until it is reset with another <FONT COLOR = ... > tag. You can use it to pick out words within normal text – though you can get strange results if you use the tags inside Headings.

R	G	B	Colour
00	00	00	Black
80	80	80	Grey
FF	FF	FF	White
00	00	80	Navy Blue
00	00	FF	Blue
00	80	00	Green
00	FF	00	Lime
80	00	00	Maroon
FF	00	00	Red
00	80	80	Turquoise
80	00	80	Purple
80	80	00	Olive
00	FF	FF	Aqua
FF	00	FF	Fuchsia
FF	FF	00	Yellow

```
<HTML>
<HEAD>
  <TITLE>My Gnome Page</TITLE>
</HEAD>
<BODY BGCOLOR = "#80FFFF" TEXT = "Green">
  <H1>Welcome to my Gnome Page</H1>
  <FONT COLOR = "Red">
  <H2>Gnomic sayings</H2>
  <FONT COLOR = "#FF8000">
  <P>Every gnome should have one.</P>
  <P>There's gno place like Gnome. (Old Alaskan proverb)</P>
  <P>Gnome is where the heart is.</P>
  <FONT COLOR = "Blue">
  <H2>Gnome computing</H2>
  <FONT COLOR = "Fuchsia">
  <P>Lots of links to go here!</P>
  <FONT COLOR = "#000040">
  <H4>This page is under construction</H4>
  <ADDRESS>Ingrid Bottomlow </ADDRESS>
  <ADDRESS>Last Update: Mudday of this week</ADDRESS>
</BODY>
</HTML>
```

Pale Aqua – the extra 80 Red makes it lighter

Orange – reducing the green from FF makes it darker (yellow = FFFF00)

Very dark blue

Tip

You must have a good contrast in shade – as well as in hue – between your text colours and the background colour. Some of these in this example are too close together for easy reading.

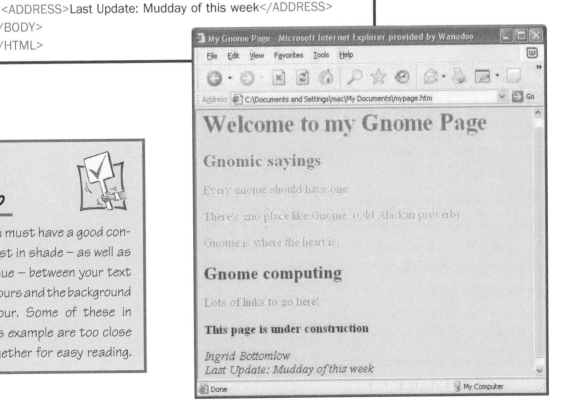

Lists and lines

Here are two more ways to enhance the appearance of your pages, without adding to download time.

Lists

These come in two varieties – bulleted and numbered. Both types are constructed in the same way.

◆   <OL> </OL> (ordered/numbered) or <UL> </UL> (unordered/bulleted) enclose the whole list.

◆   Each item in the list is enclosed by <LI> </LI> tags,

e.g.

```
<UL>
   <LI> List item </LI>
   <LI> List item </LI>
   <LI> List item </LI>
</UL>
```

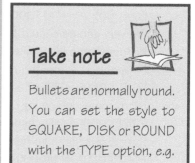

Take note

Bullets are normally round. You can set the style to SQUARE, DISK or ROUND with the TYPE option, e.g.

<UL TYPE = DISK>

Lines

Also called Horizontal Rules, these are created with the tag <HR>. This is a single tag – there is no </HR> to end it. A simple <HR> produces a thin line with an indented effect. For variety, use the options:

SIZE to set the thickness, measured in pixels. The line will normally be hollow.

NOSHADE makes the line solid.

WIDTH can also be set in pixels, but is best given as a percentage of the width of the window – you don't know how wide your readers' windows will be.

COLOR is used as in the <FONT...> tab, with the colours set by hex values or the standard names. Coloured lines are always solid, so NOSHADE is not needed.

You can see examples of all of these opposite.

```
<HTML>
<HEAD>
  <TITLE>My Gnome Page</TITLE>
</HEAD>
<BODY>
<H1>My Gnome Page</H1>
<HR  COLOR = Green>                    Simple line
<H2>Gnomic sayings</H2>
<HR SIZE = 8 >                    Thicker, hollow line
<UL>
<LI>Every gnome should have one.</LI>
<LI>There's gno place like Gnome.</LI>
<LI>Gnome is where the heart is.</LI>
</UL>
<HR SIZE = 8 WIDTH = 75% NOSHADE >
<H2>Gnome computing</H2>
<OL>
<LI>Gnome World</LI>
<LI>Seamus Sosmall's home page </LI>
</OL>
<HR SIZE = 6 COLOR = Red>
</BODY>
</HTML>
```

Unordered List

Thicker line, set to 75% of the window width

Ordered List

Solid line

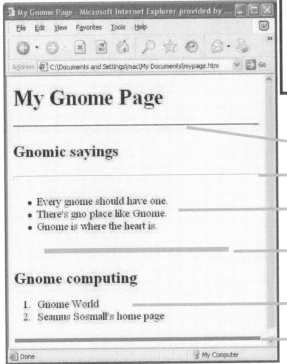

Simple line

Thicker, hollow line

Unordered List

Thicker line, set to 75% of the window width

Ordered List

Solid line

Images

There's no doubt that images add greatly to a page, but there is a cost. Image files are very large compared to text files, and even small images will significantly increase the downloading time for a page. This may not matter to people with a broadband connection, but it does to someone using a dial-up line – and a lot still do. In the example opposite, the text takes 600 bytes – almost instant downloading – while the picture is over 26Kb and will take 10 seconds or more to come in on a dial-up line. So, include images, but keep all your visitors happy by following these rules:

◆   Keep the images as small as possible;

◆   If you want to display large images – perhaps your own photo gallery, put them on separate (linked) pages and tell your visitors how big they will be.

◆   Include text describing the image, for the benefit of those who browse with AutoLoad Images turned off.

The basic image tag is:

<IMG SRC = "filename">

You can also use these options:

ALIGN = "left/center/right"
ALT = "description"

ALIGN sets the position of the image across the page.

ALT is the text to display if the image is not loaded into a browser. In the example opposite, if image loading was turned off, you would see this: ☒ A picture of me

Background images

You can add an image with the BACKGROUND = "filename" option in the <BODY> tag. The image is automatically 'tiled' – repeated across and down to fill the window.

Tip

Images must be in GIF or JPG format for browsers to be able to display them. When you are preparing images, try both formats and use the smallest.

Take note

Window's Paint can only save images in GIF or JPG format – when you save them, change the Save As type from BMP, the default format.

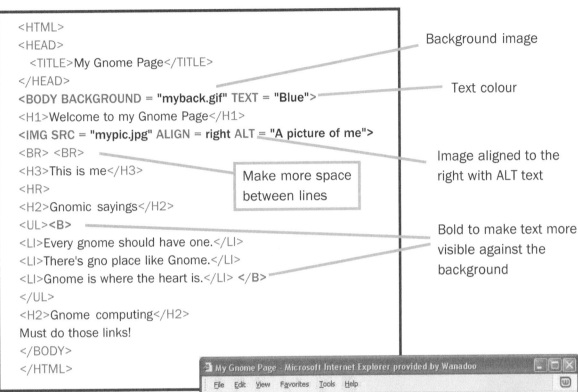

```
<HTML>
<HEAD>
  <TITLE>My Gnome Page</TITLE>
</HEAD>
<BODY BACKGROUND = "myback.gif" TEXT = "Blue">
<H1>Welcome to my Gnome Page</H1>
<IMG SRC = "mypic.jpg" ALIGN = right ALT = "A picture of me">
<BR> <BR>
<H3>This is me</H3>
<HR>
<H2>Gnomic sayings</H2>
<UL><B>
<LI>Every gnome should have one.</LI>
<LI>There's gno place like Gnome.</LI>
<LI>Gnome is where the heart is.</LI> </B>
</UL>
<H2>Gnome computing</H2>
Must do those links!
</BODY>
</HTML>
```

Background image

Text colour

Image aligned to the right with ALT text

Make more space between lines

Bold to make text more visible against the background

The trick with background images is to use one which doesn't clash too much with the text. Very pale or bright images and black text work well. In this example, the background image is the same as the main picture, but smaller and with fewer, paler colours – and if it was even simpler and paler, the text would be more readable.

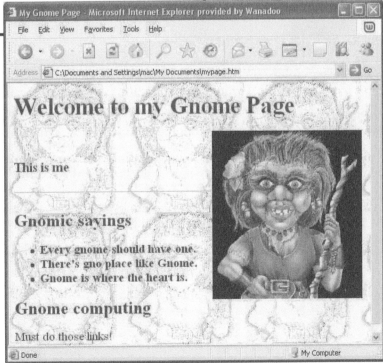

Links

A link is created with a pair of tags. The first contains the URL of the page or file to be linked, and takes the form:

<A HREF=**URL**>

The second is a simple closing tag </A>. The two enclose the image or text that becomes the clickable link, e.g.

<A HREF=http://**www.gnomeworld.gn**>Gnome World </A>

As you can see from the example opposite, the link can be embedded within a larger item of text - only '**here**' is clickable in the *IT's Made Simple* line. You can also use an image with, or instead of, text to make the link.

The example only has Web URLs, but you can equally well create links to FTP files and newsgroups. You can also add a link to give readers an easy way to contact you. This line:

<A HREF=mailto:**me@my.e-mail.address**> Mail me </A>

will open a new mail message window, with your e-mail address in the To: slot.

Links within the page

If you have a page that runs over several screens, you might want to include links within the page, so that your readers can jump from one part to another. The clickable link follows the same pattern as above, but you must first define a named place, or anchor, to jump to.

<A NAME = "Top">This is the start of something big </A>

The anchor tags can fit round any text or image, and you can even leave it blank in between if you like.

The HREF tag is slightly different for a jump.

<A HREF = #Top> Return to top of page </A>

Notice the # before the name. This is essential.

Take note

There's more to links than is shown here. In fact there is a lot more to HTML than can be covered in this book —we haven't touched forms, tables or frames. If this chapter has whetted your appetite and you want to know more, read *HTML 4.0 Made Simple*.

Tip

At some point, contact your access provider to find out what to call the home page file and where to store it and its images.

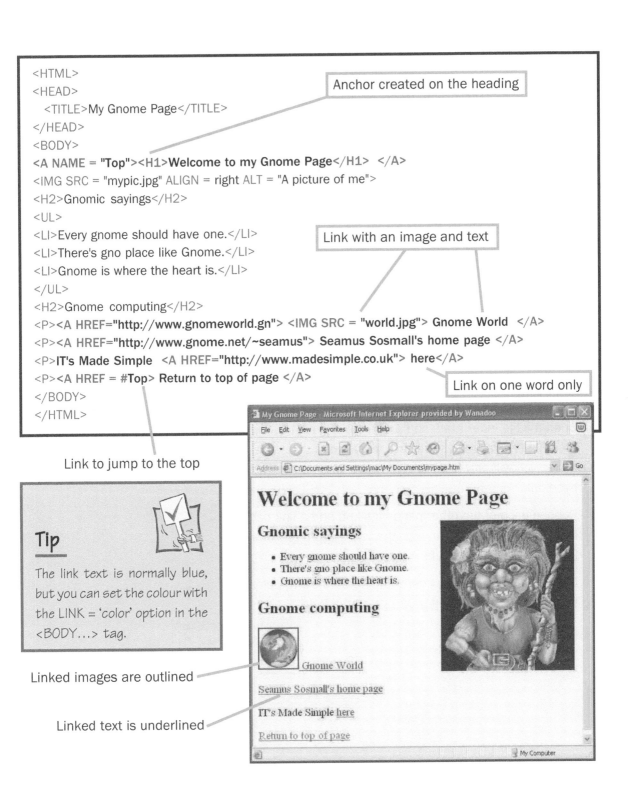

```
<HTML>
<HEAD>
  <TITLE>My Gnome Page</TITLE>
</HEAD>
<BODY>
<A NAME = "Top"><H1>Welcome to my Gnome Page</H1>  </A>
<IMG SRC = "mypic.jpg" ALIGN = right ALT = "A picture of me">
<H2>Gnomic  sayings</H2>
<UL>
<LI>Every gnome should have one.</LI>
<LI>There's gno place like Gnome.</LI>
<LI>Gnome is where the heart is.</LI>
</UL>
<H2>Gnome  computing</H2>
<P><A HREF="http://www.gnomeworld.gn">  <IMG SRC = "world.jpg"> Gnome World  </A>
<P><A HREF="http://www.gnome.net/~seamus">  Seamus Sosmall's home page </A>
<P>IT's Made Simple  <A HREF="http://www.madesimple.co.uk">  here</A>
<P><A HREF = #Top>  Return to top of page </A>
</BODY>
</HTML>
```

Anchor created on the heading

Link with an image and text

Link on one word only

Link to jump to the top

Tip

The link text is normally blue, but you can set the colour with the LINK = 'color' option in the <BODY...> tag.

Linked images are outlined

Linked text is underlined

My Gnome Page - Microsoft Internet Explorer provided by Wanadoo

File Edit View Favorites Tools Help

Address C:\Documents and Settings\mac\My Documents\mypage.htm

Welcome to my Gnome Page

Gnomic sayings

- Every gnome should have one.
- There's gno place like Gnome.
- Gnome is where the heart is.

Gnome computing

Gnome World

Seamus Sosmall's home page

IT's Made Simple here

Return to top of page

My Computer

Exercises

1 Create a text-only page to act as the top page of a web site. It should have at least two levels of headings and either bold or italic or both in the body text. The text should show the name of the site, and what it is about. Save the page as *index.html*.

2 Create a new page, giving brief details – real or imaginary – about you, the site builder. Apply colour to the page background, one of the headings and a block of text. Save the page as *aboutme.htm*.

3 Create a new page, headed 'My Pet', and insert a picture of an animal (it doesn't have to be a cat, there are already millions of photos of pet cats on the Web!). Save the page as mypet.htm.

4 Create a new page headed 'Places to see', and set up a list containing hyperlinks to half a dozen places on the web that you think other people might enjoy. Save the page as 'links.htm'.

5 Open the file index.html, and add a set of links to your other pages. As long as they are all saved in the same folder, you will only have to give their filenames in the hyperlink.

6 Reopen each of the other page files and add a link back to index.html at the bottom, with the text 'Return to Home Page' or something similar.

7 Consult your service provider and find out how to upload the files so that your pages can go on the Web.

Take note

Web pages can be called anything you like and have the extension .htm or .html. However, the top page of a site must normally be called index.html. Check with your internet service provider before uploading the files.

Index